Denis Guiney

HISTORICAL ASSOCIATION OF IRELAND

LIFE AND TIMES

NEW SERIES

General Editor: Ciaran Brady

Now available
Thomas Kettle by Senia Pašeta
John Mitchel by James Quinn
Denis Guiney by Peter Costello

Titles are in preparation on Arthur Guinness,
John Charles McQuaid and Isaac Butt

Denis Guiney

PETER COSTELLO

Published on behalf of the
Historical Association of Ireland
by

UNIVERSITY COLLEGE DUBLIN PRESS
PREAS CHOLÁISTE OLLSCOILE
BHAILE ÁTHA CLIATH

2008

First published 2008 on behalf of the
Historical Association of Ireland
by University College Dublin Press

ISBN 978 –1–906359–14–0
ISSN 2009–1397

University College Dublin Press
Newman House, 86 St Stephen's Green
Dublin 2, Ireland
www.ucdpress.ie

CIP data available from the British Library

*The right of Peter Costello to be identified as
the author of this work has been asserted by him*

Typeset in Bantry, Ireland in Ehrhardt by Elaine Burberry
Text design by Lyn Davies
Printed in England on acid-free paper by
MPG Books, Bodmin, Cornwall

CONTENTS

LIST OF ILLUSTRATIONS

FOREWORD

Originally conceived over a decade ago to place the lives of leading figures in Irish history against the background of new research on the problems and conditions of their times and modern assessments of their historical significance, the Historical Association of Ireland Life and Times series enjoyed remarkable popularity and success. A second series has now been planned in association with UCD Press in a new format and with fuller scholarly apparatus. Encouraged by the reception given to the earlier series, the volumes in the new series will be expressly designed to be of particular help to students preparing for the Leaving Certificate, for GCE Advanced Level and for undergraduate history courses as well as appealing to the happily insatiable appetite for new views of Irish history among the general public.

Ciaran Brady
Historical Association of Ireland

PREFACE

I am grateful to the editorial board of the Historical Association of Ireland, through Eugene Doyle, for the original invitation to write this book. I hope that it will go some way towards enlarging the outlook of readers and students to some non-political dimensions of Irish history.

The text of this book draws in part on the research for an earlier book that I published in 1992 in conjunction with Tony Farmar, and I would like to acknowledge the benefit derived from the research and discussions during the time we were working on the book. Mr Arthur Walls, on behalf of Mrs Mary Guiney, placed at our disposal what survived of the records of the store, and what information could be released relating to Denis Guiney, and I would like to thank him and Mr Frank McAuliffe for their information and advice. Other members of the staff of Clerys and Guiney's over the years were also of assistance. I should add, though, that the private papers of Denis Guiney were and are still not available, and that many of the private records of the companies which preceded his own have either been lost since 1853 or are not open. However, much new material, both from private sources and in the public domain, has been added to the story in the years since, and I am again grateful to Tony Farmar for the opportunity to carry out further research into the commercial history of Dublin for a history of Arnotts which he published more recently, and for the discussions which we have had on Irish commercial history over the course of several other projects. This book dealing as it does in large part with aspects of Irish history since the 1890s has also benefited by my research for other books both by myself and by friends and associates.

I am also grateful to the authors mentioned in the notes and bibliography for their information and insights on what might otherwise have been obscure matters. I am grateful to many others who, knowing of my interest in the topic, have related stories to me or directed me to new information.

I am grateful, as usual, for all the assistance received at the National Library of Ireland, the Libraries of Trinity College, Dublin, the Central Catholic Library, the National Archive, the General Register Office, the Companies Registration Office, the Registry of Deeds, the Gilbert Library, Pearse Street, Dublin and Glasnevin cemetery. Brendan Dempsey of Trinity College, Dublin has been of special help with the illustrations. Pictures reproduced in this book have all been taken from my own archive.

As regards the department store, which Denis Guiney bought in 1940, the present management prefer to use the form *Clerys*, though in earlier days the missing apostrophe was sometimes used. For consistency I have followed the current corporate usage.

The book has been edited for publication by Ciaran Brady, Department of Modern History, Trinity College, Dublin, and by Colm Croker, and prepared for the press by Barbara Mennell and Noelle Moran at the UCD Press, to both of whom I am also most grateful for smoothing out the path of the reader.

Peter Costello
Dublin, August 2008

CHRONOLOGY OF GUINEY'S LIFE AND TIMES

1893
19 January W. E. Gladstone introduces Second Home Rule Bill in House of Commons.

9 September Denis Guiney born at Knockawinna, Brosna, County Kerry, eldest son of Cornelius Guiney, a farmer.

Second Home Rule Bill defeated in the House of Lords.

1897
Queen Victoria's Diamond Jubilee celebrated in Ireland.

1898
Department store, formerly McSwiney & Delanys, founded 1853, acquired by Lombard and Murphy interests, and renamed Clerys, becomes a limited company.

1901
22 January death of Queen Victoria.

31 March census shows Irish population has declined to 4,458,775.

1905
Sinn Féin founded by Arthur Griffith and others.

1908
22 June Denis Guiney, aged 14, is placed in relative's shop in Killorglin, County Kerry, the earliest date on which he could leave school.

1911
2 April census shows Irish population has declined to 4,381,951.

October Guiney moves to Messrs O'Connor's in Kilrush, County Clare.

1912
29 February joins Michael O'Leary's staff in Killarney, County Kerry.

1913
Ulster Volunteers and Irish Volunteers founded.

August–September Dublin lockout; employers led by William Martin Murphy, owner of Clerys.

1914
Third Home Rule Bill passed.

Nineteenth annual Oireachtas held in Killarney. Irish Volunteers parade with fixed bayonets.

4 August Great Britain declares war on Germany; outbreak of the First World War; Home Rule Act for Ireland suspended for the duration of the conflict (then thought likely to end in months rather than years).

1916
24 April republican clique, supported by Germany, engineers Easter Rising in Dublin; Clerys store, having been looted, is burnt down.

1917
July Guiney moves to Dublin and begins work in Roberts & Co. of Grafton Street.

Population of Dublin approximately 300,000.

1918
Employed as traveller in west and south of Ireland by Wolsey, leading English woollen goods manufacturers.

11 November ceasefire in Great War.

December general election sees overwhelming victory of Sinn Féin in Ireland.

1919
21 January meeting of First Dáil in Dublin.

Anglo-Irish War begins with ambush at Soloheadbeg, County Tipperary.

Increasing tension and incidents of violence.

1920

January 'Black and Tans' formed.

23 February curfew (later extended) introduced in Dublin.

Guiney moved by Wolsey to Dublin area; involved with Michael Collins. Migrates to Leicester, England, to work for a drapery firm for a period.

21 November 'Bloody Sunday' in Dublin, with killing of British intelligence officers and retaliation on crowd at Croke Park.

10 December martial law declared in Kerry (also in Counties Cork, Limerick and Tipperary).

1921

Beginning of post-war economic slump.

April Guiney returns to Dublin; stays with Crowley relatives on the Howth Road.

6 May opens his own shop at 79 Talbot Street in city centre.

13 June marries Nora Gilmore.

8 July truce in Anglo-Irish War (operative from 11 July).

6 December Anglo-Irish Treaty signed in London.

1922

14 January Provisional Government of Irish Free State appointed by the Dáil.

28 June Provisional Government troops attack the Republican garrison in Four Courts, beginning open fighting in the Civil War.

5 July Guiney's shop destroyed in engagement between Provisional Government forces and Republican insurgents.

6 December inauguration of Free State government.

1923

Talbot Street shop enlarged and reopened.

May Civil War peters out.

1926

Census shows population of Irish Free State at 2,971,992 – a decline of 5.34 per cent on 1911; population of Dublin increased to 316,471.

16 May de Valera launches Fianna Fáil party, which Guiney will later support.

1927

Creation of Electricity Supply Board, and start of Shannon Scheme, leading in time to rural electrification and increased industrialisation.

11 August Fianna Fáil party take their seats in the Dáil, as a consequence of assassination of Kevin O'Higgins.

1929

5 January death of Guiney's father Cornelius at Brosna.

21 October Shannon hydroelectric scheme begins operations.

29 October collapse of share values on New York Stock Exchange leads to worldwide economic depression in following years.

1931

Guiney buys out leases of 80 Talbot Street and further enlarges premises, increasing the number of departments.

1932

9 March de Valera comes to power, having been elected government leader in Dáil.

Protective tariffs introduced; beginning of 'Economic War' with UK.

Further extension of departments in Guineys. Profile of Guiney in *Irish Industry*, praising his twelve years' progress.

1933

Guiney sells his house to Gerald Boland of Fianna Fáil; moves to Auburn, a mansion on Howth Road.

1936

27 May inaugural flight of Aer Lingus.

Population of Dublin 467,691.

1937

New Irish constitution comes into effect.

1938

10 March death of Guiney's first wife, Nora.

19 October marries second wife, Mary Leahy.

1939

September general war breaks out in Europe; petrol rationed.

1940

Guiney agrees to buy bankrupt Clerys from receiver.

28 November grand reopening sale at Clerys.

11 December conflict becomes world war with Axis declaration of war on United States, after Japanese attack on Pearl Harbor.

1941

January issue of *The Bell*, edited by Sean O'Faolain publishes important interview with Guiney.

August establishes new company, Clerys (1941) Ltd, then the largest private company in Ireland.

10 September completes purchase of Clerys with cheque for £230,000. United States troops now stationed in Northern Ireland.

German bombs fall on Dublin.

November special 'Clerys Supplement' published by *Irish Industry* as tribute to Denis Guiney.

1941–7

Publication of *Guiney's News*, as wartime advertising medium for his stores.

1942

Wartime restrictions on imports; rationing of coal, petrol and oil, and other essential items; further food rationing.

Loan from Munster and Leinster Bank to make improvements at Clerys.

1943

Increased difficulties for Irish industries; sharp rise in cost-of-living index
General election won by Fianna Fáil.

1944

Snap general election won by Fianna Fáil
Further increased difficulties over supplies; further restrictions on
transport.

1945

8 May European war ends with fall of Berlin (VE Day).
14 August Second World War ends with surrender of Japan (VJ Day). Little
change in Ireland regarding imports and supplies.

1946

Guiney refuses offer for Clerys from British interests (perhaps anxious to
move assets from Labour-governed United Kingdom).
7 May silver jubilee of opening of Guiney's original Talbot Street store.
12 May census reveals further decline in population in Éire to 2,955,107.
15 May centenary of death of Daniel O'Connell. Guiney speaks at public
meeting in Mansion House, presided over by Archbishop McQuaid;
donates 1,000 guineas to 'Save Derrynane' Committee, of which he is
chairman.

1947

30 January bread rationing introduced in Dublin.
    Guiney's News ceases publication.
Guiney active as director of Beleir, Irish-Belgian import–export company
with offices in Dublin and Brussels.

1948

February Fine Gael and allies form first inter-party government.
March first national wages agreement.
21 December Republic of Ireland Act leads to declaration that Ireland is a
Republic (18 April 1949).

1949

College of Industrial Relations founded, a reflection of concerns about social justice in business.

1950

25 June outbreak of Korean War.

7 December strike by bank officials begins, with serious effects on business in Republic (ends 16 February 1951).

Guiney's portrait included in gallery of 64 Irish national notables in the *Capuchin Annual*, of which he is a life patron.

Closure of Beleir shop at 16 Talbot Street, premises taken over by nephew as D. Guiney, Ladies and Gents Outfitters.

1951

Fianna Fáil returns to government.

21 December Córas Tráchtála established to promote Irish exports.

1952

14 June Social Welfare Act.

1954

Second inter-party government formed.

1955

16 October Seán Lemass, shadow Minister for Industry and Commerce, gives his key 'Clerys Ballroom Speech', outlining scheme of new economic development for Ireland.

14 December Ireland joins United Nations.

1956

30 May T. K. Whitaker appointed Secretary to Department of Finance.

Hungarian rising suppressed.

Guiney & Co. converted into limited company.

1957

Fianna Fáil returns to government; Seán Lemass Minister for Industry and Commerce.

October first earth satellite launched by USSR; others follow from USA.

1958

28 October election of Pope John XXIII

December T. K. Whitaker's *Economic Development* plan (arising from Lemass's Clerys speech) published by government.

Beleir ceases trading as import–export company.

1959

17 June de Valera elected President and leaves active politics.

23 June Seán Lemass appointed Taoiseach; begins vigorous implementation of new economic policies.

1960

July Irish troops deployed with United Nations in Congo.

August Denis Guiney draws up his last will.

31 December RTÉ begins television service in Republic.

1961

Census shows population of Ireland has reached lowest point in modern history; population of Dublin now over 510,000 and still rising.

Beleir company dissolved.

1962

6 July first edition of *The Late Late Show*, with Gay Byrne, broadcast.

11 October opening of Second Vatican Council in Rome; begins decline of public influence of Roman Catholic Church in Ireland, with strong effect on sales of clerical garments at Clerys.

1963

3 June death of Pope John XXIII.

26–29 June US President John F. Kennedy in Ireland.

22 August publication by government of *Second Programme for Economic Expansion* (Part I).

22 November assassination of John F. Kennedy.

1964

July publication of *Second Programme for Economic Expansion* (Part II).

December Derrynane Trust hands over deeds of Derrynane Abbey to the state; Guiney thanked for his generosity.

1965

14 December Anglo-Irish Free Trade Agreement (to become effective in July 1966). Guiney refuses offer of £11 million for Clerys from London group.

The mid-1960s begin important social and material changes in Ireland (in contrast to depressed 1950s).

1966

8 March Nelson's Pillar, city landmark outside Clerys, blown up by terrorists.

10–17 April countrywide events mark fiftieth anniversary of Easter Rising. Census reveals slight rise in population of Ireland (for first time since the Famine). Guiney's bankers, the Munster and Leinster Bank, amalgamates with the Provincial and the Royal Bank to form Allied Irish Banks, the first banking conglomerate in Ireland – a step in the creation of the modern banking environment in Ireland.

10 November Seán Lemass resigns as Taoiseach.

1967

11 May Ireland applies for membership of the European Economic Community.

8 October Denis Guiney dies in Dublin; tribute paid to him as leading commercial figure in modern Ireland by Seán Lemass.

2004

23 August Mary Guiney, the widow of Denis Guiney, dies in Dublin at the age of 103.

ABBREVIATIONS

Cork Hist. & *Arch. Soc. Jn*	*Cork Historical and Archaeological Society Journal*
GAA	Gaelic Athletic Association
INTO	Irish National Teachers' Organisation
IRA	Irish Republican Army
IWW	Industrial Workers of the World
KC	King's Counsel
MP	Member of Parliament
NAI	National Archives of Ireland
NLI	National Library of Ireland
NUI	National University of Ireland
RIC	Royal Irish Constabulary
TD	Teachta Dála

Introduction

This account of the life and career of Denis Guiney marks a new departure for the series of books from the Historical Association of Ireland. It is the first title to deal with an historical figure who was not in any large way associated with active politics or public affairs.

It would be wrong, however, to see Denis Guiney as a mere common citizen. He was far more than that, as I hope to show. But he is certainly a figure about whom little has been published; hence the content of this book will be more varied than has been the case with previous titles and the sources of information more disparate. In style too it is more popular than academic, but this may well be an advantage in a series which is increasingly aimed at the general reader who takes an interest in Irish history. Unlike previous subjects in this series, Denis Guiney has attracted little or no attention from historians. Though Seán Lemass's famous 'Clerys Ballroom Speech' of 1955 on the industrial development of Ireland is often cited, the role of his friend Denis Guiney in that development is not. Whatever the government might have wished for, it had to be men like Guiney, and his peers Joe McGrath, Jefferson Smurfit and Ben Dunne who made it happen. This book, then, is less a résumé of an existing body of scholarship than a preliminary sketch of what must inevitably be a much larger study of the central role of the businessman in modern Irish history.

Denis Guiney was a businessman pure and simple. Yet the effect of his career and the light it throws on the social and economic development of Ireland is of the first interest. Like many of Ireland's most successful entrepreneurs, he was a very private man. His personal papers are not available for consultation. His family and associates, from a misplaced sense of piety, have often preferred to see him as the subject of amusing stories, rather than as a subject of great historical significance. Denis Guiney, in fact, is typical of those individuals whose influence has been very great on the life of their fellow countrymen, but who are rarely, if ever, alluded to in conventional history. He is a character who would have appealed to Balzac, Trollope and Theodore Dreiser. Quiet and private, yet stubborn and determined in business, even ruthless at times, his effect on Irish life was truly revolutionary. He was one of those who brought about successfully a sweeping change in the way we live now. Politicians merely attempt to *manage* a country's way of life which men like Guiney actually *create*. If clothes make the man, as the old saying has it, the man who sells the clothes is actually selling a sense of personal, even national, identity. The drapery for a nation's front rooms, even a nation's underwear, things which Denis Guiney largely dealt with, are a very intimate part of its being, and when and how this aspect of the nation's life changed over the years says a great deal about the character of Irish society.

Guiney's life covers the transition in Irish life from the Second Home Rule Bill of 1893 to Ireland's application to join the European Economic Community in 1967; from the small country shop to the great city store; from the Catholic farmer's cabin to the great mansion in the respectable, once largely Protestant suburb; from the uncertainties of rural self-sufficiency to the far greater uncertainties of an Ireland engaged in a network of worldwide trade.

CHAPTER I

Early Years, 1893-1908

I

To the business enterprises he developed in later life, Denis Guiney brought the background and outlook of a Kerry farmer's son from some of the bleakest acres in the south-west of Ireland. Even after decades of living in Dublin, he always emphasised the importance to him of his family origins and early years.

I

The Feale river marks part of the boundary between the counties of Cork and Kerry. In a tuck of the mountains between Abbeyfeale and Castleisland, on a hill above a small valley running south into Kerry, on a tributary stream called the Clydagh, lies the little village of Brosna. An ancient settlement, it dated back to the times of St Mollang, the patron saint of the district, or so the locals liked to think.[1] This had been the O'Mahony country, and that family's mausoleum, dating from 1741, stood in the local graveyard. The river was originally the Brusna, but was renamed after the Clyde in honour of Sir Walter Scott, who visited the district in 1825.[2] Described by one topographer as 'a pleasant little town', with a population of a couple of hundred, it was distinguished from countless other little places just like it, by a Catholic parish church designed in the 1860s by the pre-eminent architect George

Ashlin.[3] This was an area where the evangelical drive of the
Church of Ireland in the early nineteenth century had scored some
successes, perhaps because the poorer Catholics hoped for some
material advantage from their conforming to the Established
Church.[4] Admiral Moriarty caused a Protestant church to be built in
Brosna in 1795, 'which fell to the ground the same night it was completed'; later the Catholic parish church was erected here.[5] Although
there was no Anglican parish church, the living, in the gift of the
Church of Ireland Bishop of Limerick, was worth some £150 a
year to a pluralist before Disestablishment in 1869, money extracted
by tithing from a poor parish with extensive tracts of bogland.[6]

Brosna was reached in those days by 'a fine wild drive' over
'fairly good sandy mountain tracks', passing through scenery very
different to the rest of Kerry: 'long sweeps of moorland, with
distant low hills'. Visitors thought 'the air of this upland district
[was] most invigorating'.[7]

Although the road to Newmarket passed along the valley of the
Feale, Brosna itself was almost a dead end, for there was a main
road in, but no real road out. To the south the road came to Mount
Eagle. To the west rose the Glannaruddery Mountains. To the east
were the Mullaghareirk Mountains, on the other side of which lay
the richer acres of County Limerick. For most young people in
Kerry at the end of the nineteenth century, the grass was far greener
on the other side of those mountains, as the high rate of both
internal and foreign emigration revealed.

The population of the barony of Trughanacmy had been 66,613
in 1841, but fell to 54,934 by 1851. The civil parish of Brosna had
held 2,871 people in 1841, falling to 2,364 a decade later. The little
village of Brosna itself had grown from a population of 109 in
1851, to 286 in 1891. But this rise was balanced by the fact that
Gneeves, as the registration district was called, had held nine
houses with a population of 67 just after the Famine in 1851, and

had peaked with fifteen houses and a population of 115 in 1881, but was now in decline, those fifteen houses now being inhabited by a population down to 94 in 1891.[8]

It was here, in the townland of Knockawinna, parish of Brosna, barony of Trughanacmy, that Denis Guiney was born on 9 September 1893, brought into the world by the local midwife, Margaret Nolan from Scalp Bridge.[9] He was baptised in the local church the following day, with Daniel Crowley and Mary Crowley standing as his godparents.[10]

His father, Cornelius Guiney, an Irish-speaker born in the early 1850s, was a small farmer, with a holding of about eighty acres.[11] It was 'an average Kerry farm', in good dairying country, however rough some of the surrounding land seemed to visitors. His mother Julia, formerly Crowley, a County Limerick woman ten or twelve years younger than her husband, was described by a friend as 'typical of the sensible, frugal farmer's wife of Kerry'. (She too spoke Irish.) The family home was a simple farmhouse of the traditional kind, of only three rooms, with the bedrooms off the main room in which the family of nine lived, worked and passed the time with neighbours, who included many other Guiney relatives who lived locally.[12]

The Guineys had long been established in this area of Kerry: Guiney's Bridge, to which they gave their name, was not far away, and records trace them back in this same district to at least the beginning of the nineteenth century. Beyond that they disappear into the obscurity of poverty. Locally the name was pronounced *Guinea*. By 1856 they held and owned a substantial acreage in the two townlands of East Brosna and Knockawinna. Not all the family or their connections were on the land: some relatives had moved on to business in the nearby towns.

The family was far from poor; 'comfortable' was the phrase that neighbours used. Indeed, though much of the land was marginal, this general part of Kerry also had larger and better farms, mostly in dairying, than elsewhere in the county. But poverty is relative, for Cornelius Guiney was prosperous enough in the first decade of the century to employ two live-in labourers on the farm. By 1911, with Denis already gone from home and the smaller boys still at school, he could still employ a farm servant, John Nolan. But neither were the Guineys rich. There were few material comforts in the childhood home of Denis Guiney.

The Brosna area had seen a great deal of trouble during Whiteboy outbreaks of the 1820s, when it was occasionally the headquarters of some groups of those 'primitive rebels'.[13] The payment of tithes too had been a source of protest. During the Famine the districts around Castleisland and Tralee suffered terribly – in October 1846 the men of Castleisland demanded work as they could not 'bear the cries of the hungry children any longer'. Conditions in remoter Brosna were as bad. Though the opening of the new road from Listowel to Newmarket (now the R576) made the district less isolated and more tranquil, yet again in the rising of 1848, the Land War of the early 1880s, and later, during the 'Troubles' of the early 1920s, it was to be the scene of bitter conflicts between local people and both the British and the Free State authorities.

The notorious land agent Sam Hussey observed of the area around Castleisland, which was the wealthiest portion of the district covered by the Tralee Poor Law Union, that 'there was nearly as many outrages there as in the whole of the rest of the county'. It was not actual poverty, but mere trouble-making, he thought, that was responsible for the disturbances.[14]

The people of west Kerry were independent-minded folk who got what they wanted as often as not. Many of them saw themselves as in the vanguard of the national movement, in which a number of well-known Kerrymen such as Tim Harrington and his brother Harry were prominent. In a South Kerry by-election in 1872 the voters had returned a Protestant Home Ruler, Rowland

Ponsonby Blennerhasset, in preference to a Catholic Liberal.His election was an augury of the new Irish Party, and the rise of modern Irish nationalism.

Memories of these years, from the opposing point of view of the tenant farmers, were all around in stone and story for the young Guiney to see. In the centre of Abbeyfeale, for instance, stands a memorial statue to Father William Casey (1844–1907), a prominent figure in the struggle with the local landlords, which affected many townlands around Brosna. 'The national spirit in Brosna was good', recalled the revolutionary leader Batt O'Connor, an associate of Michael Collins, who was born there in 1870.

> We had evictions, and raids by bailiffs who seized the people's cattle when they could not pay the rent. Very often there were reprisals. We had boycotting and 'moonlighting,' and I remember a Company of cavalry – the Scots Greys – being brought into Brosna to protect a bailiff who was about to give evidence against some prisoners. A young girl from the district was sent to prison for assaulting this bailiff, who had been employed to dispossess the farmer for whom she worked. A farmer was imprisoned for upholding the principles of the Land League, and his neighbours planted his crops and saved his small harvest for his family.[15]

In 1879 Moonlighters (often former Fenians) raided Mount Eagle Lodge for arms, but met spirited residence from the agent of the landlord, Lord Drummond, whom they released out of admiration for his courage.[16] Such clandestine elements lingered on. At the Brosna petty sessions court in March 1882 one of the magistrates, Arthur Herbert, a landlord of Castleisland, remarked that it was a pity he had not been in command during a riot in the village, as he would have 'skivered the people with buckshot'. Three days later, on 31 March, on his way home from having cast the deciding vote against a Parnellite, then detained in Kilmainham Jail, as chairman of the Tralee Board of Guardians, he was shot dead.[17] His body was carried back to his mansion, Killeentierna House, in a common farm-cart.[18] That night eleven lambs were done to death on his front lawn as a further insult. Despite the offer of a large reward, no one was ever charged with these crimes. Such was the 'exuberant delight' in the Brosna district at this murder, as Sam Hussey's steward observed, that 'You would think, sir, that rent had been abolished and the duty taken off whiskey.'[19]

Brosna itself was disturbed not only during the Land War in 1879–80, but also by agitation under the Plan of Campaign in 1886, 1888, and again in 1896, when it was visited by no less a national personality than Michael Davitt. General Redvers Buller was imposed as a military governor, so to speak, in the autumn of 1886 to 'restore law and order' – a task he found uncongenial, as he sympathised with the farmers in their situation. The nearby village of Knocknagoshel was fondly remembered by Nationalists of the day for the banner carried to a demonstration in support of Parnell at the time of the split in the Irish Party in 1891: *Arise Knocknagoshel and take your place among the nations of the world*. The four parliamentary seats in Kerry returned anti-Parnellites in 1892, voting along clericalist lines more than two to one against the 'Chief', though in 1895 a McCarthyite in the area defeated William Martin Murphy, a supporter of Tim Healy, the leader of the anti-Parnellites, by a considerable margin.

Anti-landlord, divided on Parnell, yet strongly nationalist, the people of Kerry often seemed radical, yet they retained a very conservative outlook in other respects. They were, after all, not totally impoverished people, but people of some small substance, with the eagerness to build it up. So they could be careful and cautious too.

At the time of the Easter Rising in April 1916 Batt O'Connor recalled that coming down directly from headquarters in Dublin, he could find only two men that week who supported the Volunteers in Brosna. The rest of the people in the village looked upon the republican leaders of the Rising in the capital as 'rebels', pro-German traitors who 'were ruining the country'.[20] One of the two dissenters from this view was Aeneas C. Guiney, also of Knockawinna, a relative and neighbour of Denis's father, who would later have a career in the public service as a local income tax inspector. Aeneas Guiney, suspecting that the young O'Connor was down in Kerry 'on business', took him aside and told him confidentially: 'Look here, Batt, though you are keeping so quiet, I know you are not here for nothing. I want to tell you I have a double-barrelled shotgun, and, if there is anything doing, you can count on me.'

Although this Guiney was O'Connor's only support at that time, over the next few years opinion changed, and O'Connor emerged as Michael Collins's right-hand man in the War of Independence. Local enthusiasm of the struggle was demonstrated on the night of 5 June 1920, the same night that the RIC barracks at Moyvane was burnt down, when a well-prepared attack was launched on Brosna Barracks as well. [21] Aeneas Guiney in time became a supporter of the Treaty, yet ironically 'those in Brosna were all strong against it because it did not go far enough and secure a Republic'.[22] It was near Brosna that a Republican attack in the Civil War led to the notorious Free State reprisals at Ballyseedy (the 'Kerry tragedies') – now commemorated by an imposing memorial.[23]

II

Such was the mixed temper of the times and the varied opinions of the district when Denis Guiney was growing up. The young man carried away with him from his Kerry childhood in Brosna the outlook and enthusiasm of his native place, both in politics and in sport. 'As a young man in Kerry,' he recalled looking back over half a century, 'I played football, naturally.'[24] For here too, in these rural parishes of Kerry, the Gaelic Athletic Association had a large following and was doing much to create a new kind of national identity. Guiney shared the resolution to make something better for himself that had inspired so many Kerry patriots, the greatest of whom in local opinion was the 'Liberator', Daniel O'Connell of Derrynane.

The general social background was one of frugal self-sufficiency. Farmers grew their own food, rearing pigs for their bacon over the year and to provide an occasional Sunday dinner. They sheared their own sheep, wove the wool and made it into frieze for coats and suits. The flax they grew became linen for their wives to make up into shirts and dresses. Locally tanned leather went into boots, shoes and harnesses. In the 1831 census there were well over 50,000 weavers in Ireland, supplying the needs of the population for cloth. The census of 1891, two years before Guiney's birth, showed only 1,092 remaining. By now cloth for all kinds of uses was a manufactured item, largely imported from English mills.

Local shops, in some of which drapers supplied the imported cloth, were very much a development of the late nineteenth and early twentieth century. In 1831 less than 2,000 people described as 'clothiers' were involved in the drapery and haberdashery trade in a country of some 8 million people (1 in 4,000). In 1891 there were over 7,000 in the same trades, for a population 4,704,750 (1 in 672). In Castleisland the 'Market', in which local produce had been sold in the 1880s, had by 1927 become the 'Emporium', which locals proudly thought was as fine as any shop in Dublin. In 1911, when Denis was not long into his first job, there were some 2,773 people engaged as either employers or employees in the drapery trade. Some 1,458 of these were women, often working in family shops. Men were more usually employed in the larger and more prosperous shops, and were paid more. When Denis Guiney left the land to join the drapery trade, he was entering a relatively new but rising business.[25]

The merchant can be seen as an agent of social change, not just in selling products from his own locality or made in Dublin, but also imported goods: cottons from Manchester, woollens from Bradford, pots and pans and cutlery from Sheffield. He was for many people not just a seller of supplies, but a purveyor of a new way of life, an engine of social advance.

The arrival of the railway in Kerry was an important factor in this change: it brought in not only manufactured goods, but also Irish and foreign tourists, took out agricultural produce, and allowed a speedier escape to Dublin, Cork, or the transatlantic ships calling in for emigrants at Queenstown (now Cobh).[26] It was a country entertainment for young men to watch the old women in floods of tears as the trains took away their sons and daughters.[27] Writing of Brosna, Batt O'Connor noted: 'The emigration from our district was continuous.'[28] The money earned by emigrants in England, and more especially in America, would for decades to come be an important element in the rural economy as an invisible export.

To thrive in an era of poverty and emigration, an individual had to have exceptional talents. When his formal education started, the young Denis was quickly marked out among his fellows by his quickness at maths. 'Dinny was a great lad with the figures', a school friend recalled when asked about their days at Knockaclarig National School, a few miles to the south of his home. Each day this calculating youth walked there in his bare feet (making them so hard that in later years as a pilgrim to Lough Derg he could walk around the stations with exceptional ease).[29] There were only around twenty students at that local school. The teachers (who were changed a great deal in those days) were impressed with his abilities. When he was only in first class, the inspector, Jim Fenton, was asking questions about mental arithmetic, and little Denis constantly popped up his hand. 'I think you have a child prodigy', Fenton told the teacher, later Mrs Eileen Guiney.[30] He seems to have been a diligent scholar up to the age of fourteen, even if room for study was limited in the little house at Knockawinna.

It was a crowded home, by modern standards, but not perhaps by those of the last century in rural Ireland. To clear-eyed officialdom it was merely a third-class house; to the Guineys it was the centre of the world. Julia Guiney was the mother of two daughters and five sons. The eldest child was a girl named Hanoria (Nora), born in 1892. Denis came next, followed by Julia (1895), Timothy (1897), Daniel (1899), Cornelius (1901), and John (Jack), the last child, born in 1906.

Nora married John Collins, a farmer at Newcastle in Cork, where Mrs Guiney went to live after her husband's death. Julia (also called Sheila) married Thomas Fahy, a civil servant in Dublin, though she later opened a drapery shop under her own name in Phibsborough, at 354 North Circular Road.[31]

Denis was the eldest son in the family. He was also the brightest and most ambitious. It was soon clear that he would go further in the world than his brothers, countrymen who were content, except for Daniel, to become farmers. Cornelius farmed at Rathkeale, and Timothy at Croon in Limerick. John also farmed. Daniel later joined Denis in business in Dublin, eventually setting up his own shop at 16 Talbot Street in 1929, where he was in business for sixteen years. He died in 1945, but the firm survives. Incidentally, though the parents spoke Irish, the seven children, products of a National School education, did not.[32]

Such a background was apt to be romanticised by many nationalists, especially those of a Fianna Fáil tendency, who had escaped from it. De Valera famously eulogised its quaint charms, and said that no man should earn more than £1,000 a year. In 1931, when Denis Guiney was already well established in trade, one local writer characterised the Kerry disdain for mere money-making: 'To lead simple, healthy, hardworking, pure and honest lives, in modest comfort should be our aim, and let Jews and others of high finance wallow in wealth.'[33]

But the Guiney parents too could make the odd astute calculation of their own, as they did in wisely deciding to send their eldest son away from agricultural production and into a service industry, abandoning the frugal comforts of the cottage for the lure of urban wealth. They had seen the small farmers wrest the land from the hands of the largely Protestant landlords. Perhaps now the commanding heights of commerce might be assaulted by the sons of the farmers.

At school Denis had once been set a composition, 'What I would like to be'. Drawing on his admiration for his shopkeeping relatives, he wrote that he wanted to be a draper, for he knew he would get a good start in life straightaway. For Denis, the small farm at Knockawinna could only be a beginning, never an end in itself.

CHAPTER 2

The World of Work, 1908–21

I

On 22 June 1908, at the age of fourteen,[1] the earliest age he could leave school, Denis Guiney was placed with a relative of his mother's, William Crowley, who ran a drapery shop in Killorglin, on the other side of the county.[2] Here Denis served his time, learning much of the practical side of the drapery business. He was not, as was the custom, actually paid anything. Mr Crowley, though only in his thirties, was old fashioned: 'strict as a jailer, kind as a mother', it was later said. The apprentices in those days lived with the family, above the shop at 2 Market Road (now Street). Denis Guiney was always deeply grateful for the years he spent with the Crowleys. William's wife Bridget, ten years younger than he was when they married in 1909, lost the two children born to the couple in the two years Denis was with them. She may well have expended her mothering on Philip O'Connor and James Lyons, the other assistant drapers, and on Denis.[3] She had help in the house from a living-in domestic, Julia O'Shea.

Indeed, Denis might not have found it so attractive in Dublin, where openings were harder to find, and where a peculiar kind of urban snobbery meant that some shops would only employ those who had done their time in other large Dublin shops.

The shop in Killorglin was in a large nine-roomed house, a first-class building, with ten windows on its frontage. The house stood in the town centre, beside the market and the courthouse. It is an indication of the style of the shop that Crowley also kept a milliner, Alice O'Donnell, then in her mid-twenties, who had been born in the far more prosperous, and therefore more sophisticated, town of Waterford. Her job would have been to see to the fashionable needs of the local ladies – this was not a shop, perhaps, for the wives of small farmers, but for a slightly more prosperous town clientèle.

Though in a pretty and picturesque situation, at the head of the Iveragh peninsula, Killorglin was nevertheless a poor place, even though a market town, famous worldwide for its annual Puck Fair (held on 11–13 August), during which a wild billy-goat, brought down from the local hills, is crowned; a curious folk ceremony which may be prehistoric in origin.[4] As Denis found, the scene was hectic during these three days, with the streets crowded with people and horses, traders selling ready-made suits, brogues and boots from the backs of carts, and an itinerant theatre with a clown show (admission one penny), confectionery stalls and peep-shows, and, above all, cattle trading. Among the banners and bunting that surrounded the goat on his high trestle could be seen the changing moods of the country, from Irish Party green flags and the American Stars and Stripes, changing to Sinn Féin tricolours and, by the summer of 1921, even a Soviet red flag. If they went nowhere else, people from the remote, often Gaelic-speaking, districts of Kerry were sure to visit Killorglin at least once in a lifetime for the Puck Fair.[5]

Though a stop on the celebrated 'Ring of Kerry', Killorglin was not a place with many attractions for the tourist, aside from a certain amount of fishing. The town itself had then a population of little more than a thousand people, which had fallen since 1891. Since the coming of the co-operative creameries in 1894 there had been an improvement for some farm incomes, but not all. What William

Crowley could hope to sell to such a financially constrained and conservative market was limited – milliner or not. Here salesmanship of a personal kind counted for a great deal. Much of what the customers did buy was bought on credit. They paid their bills when they sold their cattle or crops in season. If money was short, the bills went unpaid.

The story is told of Guiney slipping into a local pub near the shop for a quiet drink, and attempting to put his pint 'on the slate'.

'No tick,' said the landlord, taking the twopence out of the till and handing it to him. 'I'll lend you the money and you can pay me back. But no tick.'

Was it from these early experiences that he took his own 'No credit, cash only' view of trade?[6]

Because of its commercial restrictions, Killorglin was a place with a limited future for a young man like Denis Guiney. A term for apprentices was usually seven years. But after three and a half years Denis became restless and sought a new position.

In the autumn of 1911, when he had just turned eighteen, he moved on to Messrs M. O'Connor & Co. ('Drapers, Milliners and Dress Makers') in Kilrush, across the Shannon on the coast of Clare, as a buyer.[7] Although he was very young for a post of such responsibility, he was already well up to it. The population of the town was just over 4,000, and the shop situated at 1 Market Square was in a central location. The town also supported two newspapers, which carried notices of its shops and services over a wider area.[8]

Kilrush, served by the South Clare Railway, was a summer resort town, with a different, if largely seasonal, class of clientèle for its shops than Killorglin.[9] It had risen in popularity since the 1880s as a holiday resort, but did not rival the more crowded Kilkee, to the west on the Atlantic. Kilrush was the second town in Clare after Ennis, and it was where the steamers from Limerick stopped with tourists in summer, to continue their travels in Clare. The town still depended on its market, and on the harbour and its shipping and the fishing undertaken by local boats. The shop trade was better than Killorglin but still with severe limitations. O'Connor's establishment was a step up again, for it was actually a limited company, rather than a family firm.[10] But Guiney was there for only six months. Clearly a competent young man, Guiney must have been unhappy with his employer. Though Kilrush had only a small population, there was a great deal of competition from smaller drapery stores, and this must have affected the volume of business that O'Connor's could do.

So on 29 February 1912, now aged eighteen, Denis Guiney returned to his native county, taking up employment in Michael O'Leary's long-established shop in Killarney. The shop was situated in the main town in Kerry and the centre of the great tourist industry based on the Lakes of Killarney and the Macgillycuddy Reeks rising above them, which had developed since the 1830s. The Catholic cathedral was a remarkably fine building by Pugin, but commentators had always found the town, with a population of 5,500, over-filled with beggars, touts, importunate guides and other petty annoyances. Indeed while the population of Kerry as a whole after the Famine fell by 20 per cent, the population of Killarney rose by the same factor.

Thomas Crofton Croker, for instance, writing in the early 1820s, noted in his book *Researches in the South of Ireland*: 'In an evening stroll through the town, the first thing that will strike a stranger is the number of idle people lounging about the streets, or standing with their backs against the door-posts of the houses.' Killarney had been visited by Queen Victoria and Prince Albert in 1861; and with the endorsement of poets and writers such as Lord Tennyson, other visitors had flocked to see the lakes and mountains nearby. None thought much of the town, however, a large part of which was the property of the Earl of Kenmare. There was little or no

industry, apart from the small woodworking factory founded by
Lady Kenmare where the famous Anton Lang of Oberammergau
taught the locals some of his woodcarving secrets. The town
depended almost entirely on the benefits provided by the visitors.
Though they brought it a specious prosperity of a kind, there
remained large numbers of unemployed. (It was, however, noted
with surprise that the introduction of the old age pension in 1908
had removed large numbers of the beggars from the streets.) Other
Kerry people spoke ill of the townspeople of Killarney, but they
had a developed skill in dealing with tourists. Even today, notes
T. J. Barrington, the visitor can 'enjoy the ritual of being given
discount in the drapers' shops'.[11]

This was just what Denis Guiney revelled in. The O'Leary
shop was in the Arcade, at 2 Henn Street (now Plunkett Street) on
the corner with College Square. Though off the main shopping
street of the town, the street led back to the railway station and the
Great Southern Hotel.[12] The shop, which sold drapery and mil-
linery, was a large one, in a double-fronted house with some thirteen
rooms, where a staff of five or six was kept. Michael O'Leary, then
in his mid-fifties, had been married for 22 years and was well set up.
Though the town was larger, the shops were more varied (for
instance, many sold fancy goods and souvenirs to the tourists),
while the number of rival drapery firms was limited.

Here Denis settled for some five years, passing his late teens and
early twenties there. As the woollens buyer he was paid, he later
recalled, the sum of £30 a year, with his board and lodging. The
conditions for the staff were good, Mrs Margaret O'Leary, then in
her late forties, feeding them the same food as her own family of
two. O'Leary's trade being of grander kind than Crowley's, Denis
would have had a great deal more to learn about the drapery
business. It was here that his developing skills as a salesman matured
finally. O'Leary's had also the advantage of being near his relatives

in Killorglin and his immediate family a little further away at Brosna. He might quite easily have passed his entire working life in such a place. He was sometimes reprimanded for staying out late to play cards, but he was able to take out of his jacket pocket a sheaf of orders which he had garnered from those he played with.

Compared with other Irish towns, Killarney had a certain amount of sophistication because of the tourist trade. The foreign visitor brought young people like Denis Guiney, country-bred and reared, into direct contact with foreign mores and styles. It was also popular with Irish visitors of all kinds. In the summer of 1914 Killarney was host to the nineteenth Oireachtas, an annual festival of Gaelic culture, during which 'the tourist and tripper resort was transformed into the stronghold of the Gael'.[13] A hurling match between the Redmonds and Thurles attracted over 12,000 people – the largest crowd ever assembled in Killarney. There was piping, poetry, drama, dancing, and a flower show. But a feature of the occasion was a parade of 2,500 Volunteers from all parts of Kerry, who escorted the Gaelic League president, Dr Douglas Hyde, with rifles and fixed bayonets. The unit from Tralee was especially admired; it was whispered that they were all ex-military men. 'So much the better when the crisis comes', wrote one commentator, 'History may repeat itself in the descendants of Sarsfield's stalwarts.'[14] For the young draper there was perhaps an important fashion note: at the dance that followed the official reception 'the Irish costumes worn by a large number of the ladies attracted general admiration, so graceful and simple were they, doing equal justice to middle-age and youth'.[15] After Brosna, Killorglin and Kilrush, Killarney was certainly broadening for a young man's horizons.

Back in Brosna too there were echoes in August 1914 of the wider world when Batt O'Connor addressed a local parish meeting called to express sympathy to The O'Mahony, a leading Nationalist

MP, on the tragic death of his son, formerly Cork Herald of Arms, in a shooting accident. So during that significant summer the rival political moods of Ireland were clearly visible to the young Guiney.

Denis, now aged 23, was ambitious and ever anxious to advance himself, to answer the call of the wider world, to find a place for himself in the 'new Ireland' everyone was talking about that summer of 1914, in expectation of the Home Rule Act coming into force in the autumn. However, the coming war clouded the scene, postponed Home Rule, and helped foment the crisis that Irish rebels hankered for. That came with the Easter Rising of 1916, echoes of which reached Kerry, not only with the arrest of Sir Roger Casement at Banna Strand in Kerry, but with the visit of Batt O'Connor to Brosna to sound out public opinion in the village.

The war presented new opportunities for many people, not least for Denis Guiney. In the early summer of 1917 he and his close friend John Flynn took one-way rail tickets to Dublin, leaving Kerry behind them. The railway which brought so much benefit to the county by way of the tourist trade also drained away its sons and daughters. For the two young men, as for so many neighbours' sons, there was no turning back.

'I can always remember the first time I came to Dublin', Denis Guiney recalled in 1965. 'The first Monday in July, the year after the Rising, it was. I went hunting for a job, and I got one the following Thursday, in Grafton Street, with Roberts & Co.' The date was 4 July – American Independence Day.[16]

II

Founded in 1904 by Robert Holmes as a single shop, Roberts & Co. had grown over the years into a large and prosperous firm, occupying three shops, numbers 80, 82 and 83 Grafton Street (on either side of Johnson's Court). As well as linens, shoes and other goods, the store sold imported furs, a rather lavish item, suggesting their up-market clientèle. Denis Guiney's time in Roberts was to leave him with impressions which would affect the style of his own shops later on. He was particularly impressed by the furs which Roberts sold. Later the fur department in Clerys had a national reputation in the 1950s.[17]

The summer sale had just started in linens at Roberts & Co., and Holmes was prepared to give the young man a chance. He was given one day's trial, and at the end of it had achieved such a level of sales that he was formally hired. The selling skills of Denis Guiney must have already been highly developed, particularly in view of the fact that he had never handled linens before. The money was good too, he recalled. '£2 10s a week and 6d in the pound commission after that. I made £14 on commission alone in the one week. That was great money in those days.'

He stayed with Roberts for eighteen months. Although Dublin had suffered some £7 million worth of damage during the Rising and was still scarred by ruins in the city centre, the Great War had brought to Ireland a heady rush of prosperity. Grafton Street was the most fashionable street in the city, 'the Oxford Street or Bond Street of Dublin' in the view of a contemporary guide book.[18] Here the styles of London and Paris, and now even of America – for already the influence of early Hollywood was bringing into Ireland a different notion of glamour – reigned supreme. For those with an old-fashioned point of view, silk stockings and cigarettes were the ruinous novelties of the day for young women. The Jazz Age was on its way.

Living in the city was a great change for Guiney. Never one to discuss his deepest feelings, we must assume that his outlook and opinions were typical of his contemporaries. He was religious, as were many young men then, but religion was not a subject for male conversation: that was for priests and women, even in up-to-date Kerry, or up-to-date Ireland. The veteran journalist William O'Brien, who had observed every change in the country since the 1870s, returned to Dublin from a visit to Killarney and attempted to characterise the mood of the country in the summer of 1919:

> It is the day of youth, hope, pleasure, high spirits – of a *droit au bonheur*, a revolutionary 'right to happiness, the demand for a minimum wage, of joy in life, which has burst forth with the impetuosity of a torrent pent up during many centuries of degradation and subjection – combined at the same time with a religious passion which surrounded Killarney with a chaplet of churches, convents and monasteries beyond the dreams of the founders of Inisfallen or even Muckross Abbey and with a capacity for joyous self-sacrifice for the first bugle of the morning of battle as for the revel of the mess-tents.[19]

Something of this sense of mingled enthusiasms will have affected Denis Guiney in his own journey from Kerry to Dublin.[20]

In the course of his working day Guiney was accustomed to do the rounds for Roberts, visiting the hotels and other institutions, which had large orders for linens on a regular system of replacement. Then, towards the end of 1918, a friend in the trade who had wider contacts, recommended him for a position as a traveller with the Leicester knitwear and hosiery firm of Wolsey.

Starting in January 1919, Guiney travelled the west of Ireland for a year, then the south of Ireland, eventually being given Dublin as his territory by the second year. Though Wolsey, who had no offices in Ireland then, gave him a great opportunity, later Guiney would have difficulties with this firm, by then Sunbeam Wolsey of County Cork, over his own sales techniques, and they would refuse to supply him.[21]

Having served his time as Wolsey's Irish representative, Guiney was transferred to the firm's headquarters in Leicester. Leicester was a completely new and different experience for the young man. Here was the centre of the British industrial heartlands of the west midlands. Some ninety miles to the north of London, it stood on the banks of the Soar. The population was over 200,000 people. (Dublin then had a population of approximately 304,802, with 371,936 in the Greater Dublin area.) Though it was known for its boots and shoes, cottons and machinery, it had been the main centre of the British hosiery trade since the eighteenth century, and was an advanced industrial town.[22]

Life in England was a great contrast to what he had known either in Kerry or in Dublin. In Leicester Denis learnt a great deal in a few months and made personal contacts that would serve him well in later years. The power of British enterprise was all around, impressive in its wealth. But although his move to Leicester would have appeared to his new employers as promotion for the young Irishman, a career in England was not what Guiney wanted, and he soon gave up the position. Though ambitious, he may also have been a little homesick.

III

On returning to Ireland in April 1921, just on the eve of the truce in the Anglo-Irish War in July, Denis Guiney found the country a changed place as a result of the Great War and the internal 'Troubles'. Turmoil and discontent were sweeping post-war Europe, and in Ireland had taken the form of a revolution, fuelled in part by returned soldiers, to cast off the old British regime and establish once and for all an independent Ireland, in line with the other new nations emerging from the crumbling empires across the continent. Fighting had begun early in 1919, but it was not until the last months of 1920 and early 1921 that the worst effects of it were experienced in Dublin, with daily curfews, shootings, bombings and murders.

The mastermind behind the struggle was Michael Collins, and Denis Guiney was among the many people credited with acting as a courier and intelligence-gatherer for him, perhaps in those years when he was a traveller for Wolsey, a reputable British firm in the eyes of the authorities. Here the connection of Batt O'Connor, one of the most successful men so far to emerge from their native village of Brosna – he was by now a well-established builder and contractor in Dublin – with his cousin Aeneas Guiney would have been important.[23] Much of Collins's political and intelligence work was carried out over drinks in hotels and pubs, in the sort of easy informal company that Guiney enjoyed as well.

According to the Kerry journalist Shaun MacManus, Denis Guiney was once arrested by the British and searched. They found nothing. When he got back to Dublin, the boys at the IRA head-quarters were teasing him about where he had hidden the dispatch. 'If they had found it, Dinny,' Michael Collins observed, 'you wouldn't be here to laugh about it.'[24]

A commercial traveller, of course, roaming the countryside by train and car on legitimate business would be an ideal intelligence operative, well placed to observe police and military movements and to pick up gossip and rumours in shops, pubs and hotels. But it is difficult to think that Denis Guiney played any very large or significant role in the independence movement, even though he was active at the crucial time of the conflict.

Sinn Féin ('We Ourselves'), then often mistranslated as 'Ourselves Alone', was the watchword and name of the new political movement for Irish independence in 1919. The original Sinn Féin had been a constitutional, non-violent, indeed monarchist party, but after 1916 the name, applied in contempt by Dubliners to the rebels, was gladly adopted by the Irish Republican

Brotherhood as a public name for an overall umbrella group which could draw all advanced nationalists outside the Irish Party together. It was a convenient coalition that fell apart in the Civil War.[25]

Be that as it may, Denis Guiney had been affected in his own way by the movement towards independence that was in the air. From his early teens he had never had any other ambition except to be his own boss. Now he too wanted to enjoy the sense of independence promised by the new political slogans.

CHAPTER 3

In Business for Himself, 1921-40

I

In 1921, the year in which the Truce (in July) and the Treaty (in December) brought about the creation of the Irish Free State, two very important events occurred in the life of Denis Guiney: he got married, and he opened the first shop of his own. His bride Nora Gilmore, in her twenties, came of farming stock in Mountbellew, near Moylough, County Galway, and was the second youngest of six daughters of Patrick and Mary Gilmore of Lakeview, in the village.[1] However, she was then living at 9 Spencer Street, off the North Strand, a small two-roomed cottage, strictly a lower working-class address.[2]

Denis himself, now 27 years of age, was living in superior quarters with his relatives of the Crowley family, at St Mary's, 5 Howth Road. This was the residence of Cornelius Crowley, who had come up to Dublin to work in the drapery trade before the Great War, and now owned a ladies and gentlemen's outfitters and shoe shop at 6–8 Upper O'Connell Street. Another relative, William Frederick Crowley, was in charge of the local post office on the other side of the road.[3] Yet another of these relatives, Timothy Crowley, was Denis's best man when he and Nora were married in St Laurence O'Toole's church in Seville Place on 13 June 1921.[3] They set up home in 114 St Lawrence's Road,

Clontarf, a modest late Victorian red-brick house in a very quiet neighbourhood, only a few doors away from the home of the Sinn Féin founder Arthur Griffith.

With what little she brought to the marriage – largely her shop skills – together with his own savings from his time with Wolsey and in England, and with other money borrowed from his father, Guiney looked around for a place to start up his own business and was able to lease premises at 79 Talbot Street.[4] This was only a small shop, previously run as a small drapers by a Mrs Madden, with a 24-foot frontage, and an annual valuation for rates of £25, which he and his wife were able at first to run by themselves. The building was shared with a house agent (MacArthur's, founded in 1880), a fruiterer, and show-card maker, and had once been used by other drapers and dressmakers. Beside them along the street were a butcher, a shoe shop, a small dress shop, a pub, and Prescott's dye works.[5] They had three 'departments' in the one small room. It was

1 Façade of the first Talbot Street shop, 1922

in fact little more than a small country-town shop transferred to the city centre. Nora Guiney was said in these early years to be very much its guiding spirit. As it stood it would never make a fortune, but it had one enormous advantage for Denis Guiney: it was *his* business.

At that time the drapery trade in Dublin was normally carried out in the more fashionable Grafton Street or Henry Street. Talbot Street, an inner-city shopping area in a working-class district, was not fashionable. For many, indeed, Talbot Street was disreputable because of its nearness to the notorious brothel quarter of 'Monto', nearby in Montgomery Street and Railway Street; and being near Amiens Street railway station, it was an area of small hotels and casual lodging houses. Though it had escaped destruction during Easter Week, it had earlier been the scene of a riot on 29 August 1914, during the great lockout, when the impoverished denizens of the slums clashed with the Dublin Metropolitan Police 'to the accompaniment of hoarse, ribald execrations and shrieks' until nearly midnight.[6]

These were the poor – for whom his wife had a great sympathy – who would be among Denis Guiney's first customers. Owing to war and social deprivation, property values were not high in Talbot Street. Denis Guiney thought it a good place for his kind of shop, even though it had been the scene of a notorious shoot-out between detectives and the IRA man Sean Treacy in 1920 outside No. 93 – the Republican Outfitters. But with the end of the Troubles, and a little later the closing down of Monto after vigorous action by the Legion of Mary, the district took a swing upwards. The old tenements were replaced by the corporation with blocks of flats. The shops and their businesses began to revive and prosper a little. It was a street with many long-established firms, such as Olhausens Pork Butchers, where one could buy (as in the time of James Joyce's *Ulysses*) crubeens and sheep's trotters. But it could not be called a major shopping resort. The place and the people were more characteristic of the older Dublin. A guide book of 1921, the very year Guiney opened, did not mention Talbot Street as a shopping resort; yet a generation later in 1950, in a revised edition of the same guide, it had become a 'busy domestic shopping thoroughfare'.[7] This change, so accurately described, was due largely to the presence of stores like Guiney's.

Guiney had clearly seized the right moment to start his own business. He opened his shop door, over which the fascia proclaimed 'Guiney and Co. Ladies' and Children's Outfitter', six weeks before his wedding, on Friday 6 May 1921, in time to take advantage of the influx of Saturday shoppers.

That summer was a scorching one, in the first week of July reaching 75° Fahrenheit in the shade in Dublin one day; 93° in the sun in Greystones; 89° in Malahide. Water was strictly controlled. Guiney was summoned by the city corporation for using drinking water from the Vartry system to wash the windows of the shop. In court before Sir E. Swifte KC he claimed that there must have been some mistake as he had given instructions that very little water was to be used in the shop. But the defence failed: he was fined 40s.

The little shop soon came to be talked about, as people passing noticed the good value of what was being sold. Initially the 'Good Value' on offer was all that distinguished it from many other small shops in the district. But then the citizens of Dublin were surprised by a large advertisement, a very large advertisement, in the evening papers. Already Guiney was convinced of the primary value to the modern city trader of advertising. The advertisement filled three full columns, and the items offered were at unbelievably low prices. Thus was the attention of the public drawn to the very first of the 'Guiney Sales' which would later become part of Dublin folklore.

The next morning the crowd was dense on the pavement of Talbot Street in front of the shop. Soon customers were coming in from all parts of the city. Critics in the drapery trade said his goods were either rubbish, or that he was selling at below cost. The customers knew they were getting good value, but there was some truth in this claim of selling below cost. The shop had opened in the year of the post-war slump. Prices from suppliers were falling week on week. But though money was scarce, many shops had high prices. Undoubtedly Guiney was selling quite a lot of goods under the costs of other traders, but never at less than what they had cost him. For Guiney this was the key point. He had simply bought the goods in the right market. 'I want to give the poor people value,' he was later quoted as saying, 'and the way to do it is bulk-buying.'[8]

Denis Guiney always regarded that Friday, indeed any Friday, as his lucky day, regardless of long-established Catholic tradition that it was an unlucky day. But in little more than a year disaster struck. During the terrible fighting in the city centre during the opening days of the Civil War, on 5 July 1922, Talbot Street came under fire from Provisional Government forces, and in the ensuing struggle the little shop of Guiney & Co. was destroyed.[9]

Various Republican, Communist and IWW elements had occupied Moran's Hotel across the road as a key to the city blocks they were holding. They were shelled by the Free State Army with a field gun mounted on a train on the railway bridge at the end of the street. On Saturday 1 July the auctioneers and Guiney's went on fire, two of five fires that afternoon that the fire brigade had difficulty in dealing with, as their main resources were focused on the Four Courts. The insurgents were soon driven out of Moran's Hotel which was captured (along with 30 Irregulars) at 8.30 p.m, on Sunday night.

Over a month later, as the fighting still raged across the country, Denis Guiney filed a claim with the government authorities for compensation on 19 August 1922 for £9,402 5s 6d for loss of stock and damage to the premises. In due course in May 1924 he was awarded £6,600, though a higher figure of £7,964 was also quoted at the time. (The claim on Moran's Hotel was for £20,000. Later the government party claimed that the total cost of the Civil War for which they held the republican parties responsible was over £35 m.)

On 29 September 1922, while Guiney's premises were still closed up, four employed young men tore back the boarding and entered the premises and were looting it, throwing boxes out into the street, when two policemen came on the scene and went into the shop. One was told from outside the shop to put up his hands but called out 'Police'. Someone outside shouted 'Free State' and ran away. On emerging into the street one of the young men fired on the police officers, but they were soon arrested and sent for trial. This was not an untypical event in Dublin in the last days of the Civil War.

With the hoped for government compensation, Denis Guiney was soon back in business. With MacArthur's he was 'making new plans for No. 79 Talbot Street'. He acquired the adjacent fruit shop and the premises of the showcard maker and incorporated them into his own premises, creating a new frontage with three floors above. The valuation now increased significantly to £140. He hired six and later eight staff, reopening early in 1923. The shop now had an attractive double front with a central door and six plate glass windows almost reaching the ground, ideal for displaying his merchandise. It was now proclaimed on its fascia board as *Guiney & Co., Ladies' & Children's Outfitters, Milliners & General Drapers.*[10] (The stylish exterior attracted other kinds of notice: in June a drunk was fined £45 7s 9d for maliciously breaking the plate glass. Mr Justice Dodd took a lenient view of the case when the culprit pleaded guilty and offered to pay full compensation.)

Soon his style of trading for small profits and a quick turnover made the name of the shop well known, as did his flair for promotion. 'I don't think he ever studied a textbook on commerce, accounting, or anything like that,' a friend later said.[11] Experience and his native wit were all he needed.

2 Façade of the second Talbot Street shop, 1926

The opening sale, always a special gimmick of Denis Guiney's, was again advertised across three newspaper columns. The crowds thronged the pavement the next morning. Prices were falling that year, and his fell with them. Now more than before he sought out bargains week by week from the trade and passed them on to his customers at the lowest possible margins, far lower than was customary in the drapery trade, which at that date was very conservative. Guiney concentrated on reasonable quality at the lowest prices for his customers.

His advertisements in the summer of 1923 spoke of a '£25,000 Sacrifice Sale'. Others claimed that 'no matter where you live, it will pay you well to come to Guineys'. The shop was '2 minutes from the Pillar; 2 doors from Lr. Gardiner Street'. He was ready to take advantage of every opportunity. In November imported goods held up at the docks by the protracted Labour strike begun by James Larkin were finally released. 'We have now got delivery and on account of the long delay and the fact that some of the bales were slightly damaged, we have induced the manufacturers to allow us a special discount of 50 per cent – equal to half the original cost.'

However, in a drawing of the store used in some advertisements the artist drew the motor car outside and the customers admiring the windows smaller than life size, thus creating an even more impressive view of the business.

'I started off on the right foot,' he later recalled, 'buying good stuff, cheaply and for cash. I bought in big quantities, and sold them at small profit. I did all the buying. I'd go over to England and buy thousands of lines for cash, return and sell them in my shop at just a little more than I paid for them and the customers poured in. Business just boomed after that and I was able to buy out [the leases of] the premises.'[12]

But trade was not without its difficulties. In April 1924 the shop was picketed by trade unionists in connection with a dispute over the early closing of drapers' shops. A woman picketer was bound over to keep the peace for having gone into the shops between 9 and 10 p.m. and used 'intimidatory expressions towards Mr Guiney and a number of customers'. She told the customers they should not be shopping there, and as an assistant that he should be in the union. That assistant, Richard Fox, claimed in court to be a member of the Post Office Workers Union – but this was swiftly denied by the union.

The regulations were changed so that shops had to close at 8.30 p.m. – after all even workers were entitled to some life at home. Yet on 5 November 1926 Guiney was convicted of having allowed customers in after closing time on 26 October and was fined £6. (He was not alone: on the same day two other firms were also fined.) A further court case followed in November 1924 arising from what had seemed to be a shoplifting incident in July, which led to a claim of slander by the lady in question against Denis Guiney. The action was dismissed.

Occasionally difficulties arose with his suppliers too, as was the case in May 1926 when the Klenger Company took him to court over selling seconds as if they were full goods; but this seems to have arisen from error rather than intent and Guiney continued to sell the brand. Another case arose out of goods sold to Guiney by Messers Daniels of London. He had driven a hard bargain getting the 20s coats for 10s, which he sold at 15s. But the company would not agree and sent other coats. These he said were not up to much and he refused to pay for them. In this case the court dismissed the claim. (Another case brought by Nicholson and Morrow of Belfast was amicably settled out of court in February 1932.)

More serious was a civil action for false imprisonment that had arisen out of a supposed shoplifting incident on 9 July 1929. Mrs Margaret Murphy of 20A Spencer Street – the poor working-class street off the North Strand where Nora Guiney had lived – held a club ticket and was selecting items to buy when an altercation arose with an assistant and Mr Guiney was called. He brought in a Guard and Mrs Murphy was taken to the police station. A prosecution failed and Mrs Murphy sued Guiney. Her claims of malicious prosecution and slander failed, but she was awarded £50 damages and her costs. She impressed the judge as 'a very respectable woman'. She had not committed the offence with which she was charged and Mr Guiney had no justification in giving her into custody. Actually it seems he had reasonable grounds for suspecting that an offence might have been committed and was right to call the police. Guiney's lawyers thought so too, but he lost his appeal in November.

The city would have gained from all of these cases the idea that Denis Guiney drove a hard bargain and that he was not a man to be trifled with over anything. However, a criminal case involving the fraudulent purchase of a lorry by hire purchase found Guiney signing a cheque for a third party and a hire purchase document without reading it.

Guiney was now in a position to stretch himself. In September 1927 he and Cornelius Crowley registered a company, Crowley and Co. Ltd, in which only the two of them held nominal shares.

He was also dabbling in property. Across the road in December 1928 he acquired 22–23 Talbot Street, the Talbot Furnishing Company, a natural companion to his main drapery business.

By the end of 1931 he had also taken over the neighbouring stores on the block, Nos 80 (the shoemaker and dress shop) and 80A (the butcher), and made many alterations when the last of the other tenants left. Though his previous valuation had been £140, the new shop was valued at £120, with £24 and £40 for the additional areas. He had also taken in a hall behind No. 44 Lower Gardiner Street on Beresford Lane that ran behind the rear of the shops, which had at one time been large enough to house a bicycle manufacturer.

He had the whole frontage rebuilt in the contemporary Art Deco style, with black glass panels, six large plate glass windows, and newly designed logo in fashionable Gill sans serif lettering. It had a walk-in entrance with a central display case, but the windows remained crammed with goods, for Guiney's idea of a good display was one which showed off the wonderful range of low prices he offered on the widest range of goods. He was not an exponent of the new artistic style of window dressing, such as that provided by the rising young artist Norah McGuinness for the enterprising Ned McGuire at Brown Thomas, the long-established store across the city in Grafton Street. As part of his programme of expansion, Guiney recruited additional staff, and he added on a household goods department and a men's and boy's department. For the first time he began selling ready-made clothing – this in itself a novelty in Dublin, where many men still had their suits made for them. Moreover, he offered not only exceptional value, but the goods were increasingly of Irish manufacture. The next year he added other departments: dress goods (silks and such) and footwear. A decade later the Guiney store had thirteen large departments and a staff of over fifty, later still twenty departments and a staff of a hundred.

3　The Art Deco glory of the store in the 1930s

Naturally such an enlargement drew comment and praise, and
Guiney was made the subject of a long appreciation in one of the
first issues of *Irish Industry*, the second number of which was
published in December 1932. The editor of this 'journal of Irish
business' was P. L. McEvoy of McEvoy's Advertising Agency in
Abbey Street, who handled all Guiney's advertising for many years.
McEvoy was a trenchant commentator on the business scene in
Ireland, and what he wrote had the ring of truth. Guiney, he proclaimed in unmeasured terms, had achieved the esteem of his peers:

> If we were asked what it is that has made Guineys we would say that
> there were three chief reasons:
>
> (1) keen value at all times;
> (2) always plenty of stocks;
> (3) systematised advertising;
>
> Add to these the keen business methods and dynamic energy of Denis
> Guiney (and, whisper, of Mrs Guiney too) and you get the foun-
> dations on which has been built the most spectacular retailing success
> in modern Ireland. Guineys is a business worth studying.[13]

A self-effacing man, Guiney was delighted not for his own
personal prestige, but for the reputation of the business.

The context of this praise was important. De Valera and his
Fianna Fáil party had come to power in March 1932, and though
he was dedicated to an ideal of self-sufficiency, he appointed Seán
Lemass as his Minister for Industry and Commerce, in which
capacity the young man (already marked out as the Chief's possible
successor) had begun to promote his 'industrial revival'.[14] He was
the most urban in outlook of de Valera's cabinet – his father ran a
long-established hat shop and outfitters in Capel Street – and
appreciated more keenly than most of his colleagues that the

increasing need for city jobs meant industrial development willy-nilly. Industrial employment stood at 111,000 in 1931 (up from 103,000 in 1926), but between 1931 and 1936 it rose to 154,000. This rise was almost all in manufacturing. *Irish Industry*, which promoted the ideals of manufacturing in general, was publicist McEvoy's response to the new government policy. Guiney from the point of view of both the Fianna Fáil and the trade paper was the ideal model for others to emulate if they could.

His position in Dublin and his political connections secured Denis Guiney and his wife invitations to the great State Reception at Dublin Castle that marked the Eucharistic Congress in Dublin in the summer of 1932 – one of the few times he made such a public appearance.

Guiney was not above an active role in politics on occasion. He proposed the nomination of Cormac Breathnach, a middle-aged Kerry-born teacher, native-speaker and writer, who lived in Clontarf, to stand for the North Dublin seat in the Dáil in the surprise election of January 1933. A former President of INTO and of the Gaelic League, Breathnach, who was also a member of the Corporation, would be eventually be elected Lord Mayor in 1949. Next to Gerald Boland and Oscar Traynor, he was one of Guiney's closest friends in Fianna Fáil.

All in all, Denis had succeeded, as had been hoped when he and Daniel left home. In contrast, his father, Cornelius Guiney, when he died in January 1929, had only a meagre estate of £86 to leave to his widow, and even that was not administered until November 1931.[15] (Denis's brother Daniel, who would die in May 1945, had accumulated an estate worth £5,245 to leave to his widow Esther and his children.)[16]

On the domestic scene, the Guineys began their married life in the house he had taken earlier, 114 St Lawrence's Road in Clontarf (£23 valuation). This was offered for sale with vacant possession in

July 1922 by MacArthur's Auctioneers: it was described as 'a modern residence, with sittingroom, diningroom, 4 bedrooms, bath (hot and cold), w.c., kitchen close range, 2 pantries, coalhouse, electric light, good garden front and rear; ground rent £4 10/-; lease 250 years; can be seen anytime'. It was auctioned on 28 July; No. 119 went for £924 in 1925. The Guineys completed the sale in October 1922, and moved across the road to 25 St Lawrence's Road (£27 valuation). The first house had been semi-detached with a good garden; the second, built in 1896, was double-fronted detached with a much larger garden. They bought this from its widowed owner in August 1924 – perhaps with money from the official compensation for his Civil War losses.

In September 1931 they sold this house for £1,530; and moved to 102 Howth Road, a larger and more comfortable house which he had built standing in a generous lot of land (valuation £34 10s), acquired in March 1929 from a lady who had only bought it the year before. This land was part of a subdivision of the grounds of a large house, and had an underpass for a footpath leading under the railway into the grounds of the golf club – a distinct advantage for a golf enthusiast.

Guiney in turn divided his piece into two lots, on one of which was the former gate lodge. In April 1929 he was granted building approval for two bungalows on the land at 102 Howth Road – the second being a renovation of the lodge as a small house (No. 100, valuation £20), which he sold on in April 1933 to his tenant Richard Fox, an associate in the shop.

His own house he called Denora, behind which he later added 'a motor house', a garage with accommodation for a chauffeur. This much larger Guiney home had two advantages: it was only a step away from Clontarf railway station and across the road from Phil Byrne's public house – which would be a familiar haunt of Guiney's in the decades to come.

At the end of March 1933 he sold Denora (now with a valuation of £40) for an unrecorded sum to Gerald Boland, a leading member of the Fianna Fáil executive which had come to power twelve months before, who had been living in a small working-class house in Marino (5 Brian Avenue, Fairview; £11 valuation), and now needed a residence more befitting a government minister.

This speculation on the Howth Road (part of the rapid redevelopment of the district in the 1920s) had raised the valuation of the land from a mere £9 originally in 1928 to over £60 by 1933 – a gratifying achievement which might have made him interested in other such speculative developments. But this did not come about.

By October 1933 the Guineys had settled into Auburn Villa, just eight lots away at 118 Howth Road, a veritable mansion with a valuation of £50, which would be Denis Guiney's home for the rest of his life. In a decade or so the Guineys had risen, stage by inexorable stage, from almost nothing to being near the top of the property market in North Dublin.

Auburn was a large double-fronted, five-bedroomed Italianate house, dating from 1861, almost facing the turn into St Lawrence's Road, with some two acres or so of ground and a stream at the back. It also had a period glasshouse and a gothic summer house. The only disadvantage was that the main railway line to Belfast ran immediately behind the garden wall.[17] But beyond that was Clontarf golf course which they used a great deal. And it was only a step or two further away from Phil Byrne's.

Auburn had formerly been owned by Lewis Crowe, a partner with his brother in a long-established Dublin timber merchants, a Methodist prominent in Dublin commercial life. Though Crowe moved on to a larger house on the Merrion Road in Pembroke, his replacement in Clontarf by the newly rich draper son of a small Kerry farmer would have seemed to some nationalists of that day (such as Mr Boland) as the only-to-be-expected outcome of Irish independence, the usurpation of Protestant business interests across the country by a new Catholic commercial class.

II

The population of Ireland had been in decline since the middle of the previous century. A consequence of this 'flight from the land' was the annually increasing population of Dublin. Between 1901 and 1921 it had risen by eight per cent. The population of the greater Dublin area stood in 1921 at 371,936. It would continue to rise, as the administration and industries became concentrated in the new capital, all through Guiney's life, providing him with an ever-increasing customer base.

A feature of Irish commercial life after 1924 was the effect of protective tariffs on imports. In that year the government imposed a tariff on boots and shoes. In 1925 tariffs on clothes, such as men's apparel, blankets, wooden furniture and bedsteads followed. Then, in 1926, the Tariff Commission which had taken over from the government imposed levies on woollens and worsteds and on silk-covered down quilts (the feathers for which were, of course, a by-product of the chicken-rearing industry, then coming into vogue in England). All of these items were sold in Guiney's shop. As a good nationalist, he was prepared to buy from Irish manufacturers, but there was a public perception that the quality was not as good as that of the imports, and that protected Irish industries were able to save on costs by paying lower wages. As figures from as early as 1930 demonstrated, protection had created new jobs (especially in shirtmaking, wholesale clothing, and boots and shoes). The overall economic climate in the Irish Free State under the Cumann na nGaedheal government and later under de Valera was not good, largely because of the undeveloped nature of the economy. Railway receipts for the carriage of goods, an indication of the amount of internal trade, were well reduced from the 1925 level by 1930. Emigration remained high, though this was reversed somewhat in the years of the Great Depression. Nevertheless, in Dublin, if not in Kerry, it was at least possible now for some to prosper.

The year 1932 saw the coming to power of Eamon de Valera and his Fianna Fáil party, completing in the eyes of many the final stage in the transition to independent Irish government. Denis Guiney was by now a supporter of Fianna Fáil. One of de Valera's first political moves was to refuse to pay the land annuities due to the British government under the terms of the Treaty, and this led to an 'economic war' with the United Kingdom, which further damaged the Irish economy, by reducing exports. To the horror of a farming nation, calves had to be slaughtered and the carcasses burnt, because fattened cattle could not be exported. Ireland's loss was Argentina's gain. Protectionism was to remain the gospel of Irish government for some time to come. Reliance on the state was deprecated by conservative economists. It was thought that the government had provided all the right conditions, except one. As the economist Professor George O'Brien of University College Dublin observed, 'The further condition of industrial progress, namely enterprise, must be supplied by the business community itself'.[18]

In the context of the new Ireland which had emerged since 1922, Denis Guiney, with his drive and ambition, was an outstanding man of enterprise. His store grew and grew during the 1930s, largely because money was in very short supply in the post-Depression years, and Guineys simply offered Dubliners the best value to be found. The turnover of 1931–2 was thirty times that of 1921–2; that of 1945–6, sixty times.

The shop was increasingly popular with the Dublin middle classes. Anything purchased in Denis Guiney's store was parcelled in a very distinctive green wrapping paper, immediately recognisable to all true Dubliners. Many of the more socially sensitive customers would disguise the distinctive Guiney bags, some by going into the chemist's shop next door and getting a more acceptable one there. There were stories of Guiney angrily confronting such people and refusing to allow them to be served in his store. As far as he was concerned, if his goods were the best buy in town, that was nothing to be ashamed of, even for ladies from the middle-class suburbs of south Dublin. His pride in his store knew no limits – and rightly so, many of his customers felt.

Guineys was a special resort of country people. Falling agricultural prices, the result of de Valera's economic war with Britain, meant that farmers appreciated a good bargain even more than the city folk. A feature of his service was his scheme for refunding their rail fare for any country customers who spent more than £5. Indeed, he even ran special excursion trains of his own from provincial towns to his sales. And on 8 December, the traditional day on which country people took advantage of the church holiday to come up to town to do their Christmas shopping, Guineys was descended upon annually by huge crowds buying for Christmas.

Denis's brother Dan, who had come up to work for him, left to open his own store down the road at 16 Talbot Street, in 1935. 'He did a good trade', Denis fondly recalled. 'My overflow of customers helped him a lot. I didn't mind the opposition in the least. It's all good for business, that's what I say.'

Other family matters were less happy. In 1936 Nora Guiney was diagnosed as suffering from carcinoma of the breast; and in the spring of 1938, having been nursed through her illness at home, she died on 10 March. She was, so it was claimed, only 38.[19] It had been, inevitably, a very painful passing. The funeral was well attended, with the government minister Oscar Traynor in attendance. In Glasnevin Cemetery Denis raised a large and very conspicuous memorial to her memory in a prime position close to the O'Connell Circle.

An old-fashioned Irishman, Denis Guiney could not exist without a wife at home and a helpmate in the shop. One marriage to a shop girl had turned out well, perhaps another might also? There were several younger members of his staff who it is said 'set their caps at him', and there was intense rivalry to catch the eye of Mr Guiney.[20] Within a few months (32 weeks to be exact), on 19 October 1938, in the Pro-Cathedral in Marlborough Street, Denis Guiney, then aged 45, married his second wife, Mary Leahy, then in her late thirties.[21] The speed of this remarriage, which might surprise even modern sophisticates, was something which the second Mrs Guiney strove in later years to disguise by obscuring the gap in time and her own age. It may well be that both Denis and his new wife harboured feelings of guilt about the first Mrs Guiney. Denis too was not above being a little misleading about what was after all a matter of public record: he told a journalist in 1965 that Nora had 'died years earlier'.[22]

Mary Leahy, born in March 1901, was from County Limerick. She was the daughter of John Leahy, who was (like Denis's father) a farmer, with a place at Creeves, Shanagolden.[23] Like Denis, and indeed Nora Guiney, she was part of that migration to the city which rural Ireland was passing through, making the greater proportion of Dublin's population of non-urban origin. She had been partly educated at the Dominican Convent in Eccles Street. At the time of her marriage Mary Leahy was living, as so many respectable business girls then did, in a private hotel, the *Ossory*, beside Belvedere College in Great Denmark Street. This prim respectability was a contrast to the working-class cottage from which Nora Gilmore had married 17 years before. Furthermore, the venue chosen for the wedding, with Nuptial Mass and Papal Blessing, was noticeably more distinguished than that used in 1921. It was followed by a wedding reception in the Gresham Hotel for a large party of guests, which included not only family and friends, but also Denis's political associates such as Gerald Boland TD, then Minister of Lands, and Dr Cormac Breathnach TD. The honeymoon was spent in England and on the Continent.

This quick remarriage, a bare eight months after Nora's death, was not in accordance with accepted social custom. At a time when people in Dublin wore half mourning (a black arm band or patch), or even full mourning, for a complete year after a family death, when many widowers or widows would never have contemplated marrying again, this event was certain to have caused comment, even in Dublin; and it is no wonder that in later years both partners carefully avoided alluding to the brevity of the time span between the two marriages. But here Denis Guiney was simply showing the same hard-headed outlook on life that he had displayed in the spring of 1921. Unhappily there were no children by either marriage.

Mary Leahy (like Nora Gilmore) had many years experience in the drapery trade, and though some years younger than he was, was to prove the ideal helpmate in the challenges that were to face her husband as the 1930s drew to a close.

III

The larger and the more exclusive shops in town did less well in this period, which for many of them was a time of decline. The outbreak of the European war in the autumn of 1939 made the position even more critical, and was little eased by the entry of America into the struggle, making the conflict a true world war in December 1941. The government took emergency powers on 3 September 1939, and petrol rationing was introduced on 13 September, with additional measures in January 1941. Press censorship was imposed, covering both foreign and domestic events. More vital to Guiney was the ban on wage increases.

Ireland was actually fairly comfortable during the war, being well supplied with food, if not with imports. Indeed, it was not until January 1947 that bread rationing was introduced.

At Guiney's, however, 'it had become almost impossible to find standing space in the shop during the latter half of any week, and at sale times particularly long queues of waiting customers had become the rule', recalled P. L. McEvoy, the long-time friend of Guiney's, and now President of the Federation of Irish Manufacturers, who still handled all of Guiney's publicity through his Abbey Street advertising firm.

It was at this moment, when Denis Guiney's firm was thriving, that Dublin was shocked to hear that bankruptcy and closure faced the famous old firm of Clery & Co. That news was followed by the even more sensational (though unfounded) rumour that the great Denis Guiney had bought it out, lock, stock and barrel, for £20,000. If the real price of a quarter of a million pounds had been known, it would have been thought even more sensational.

To those who knew how limited the space in Talbot Street had become and what an opportunity Clerys provided for a born entrepreneur, the purchase did not come as a surprise. The turnover for 1939–40 in Guiney's Talbot Street shop was much bigger than Clerys in the same year; by 1941 it was up to £1 million a year.[24]

Dublin waited to see what Denis Guiney ('Our Dinny') would make of the Victorian 'Monster Store' which he had captured from what some might have seen as a set of outmoded plutocrats. In the history of Clerys' department store much of the commercial development of modern Ireland since the Famine was illustrated.

CHAPTER 4

The Making of a Department Store

In his business career Denis Guiney had worked his way up through the various stages of the Irish commercial world; the small country-town store, the store in a small resort, the larger store in the county town, and finally the small and then the medium store in the national capital. His shop in Talbot Street was, in a manner of speaking, a large shop transferred from a provincial town to the city. But the next step was a greater one, for he was to take over a department store, and the department store had a special place in the worldwide development of retailing, and in the development of the Irish economy.

With the purchase of Clerys, Denis Guiney entered upon a new phase of his commercial career by acquiring a major institution in the economic life of the city, in the history of which much of the development of the Irish retailing was illustrated.[1]

I

The store traced its history back to May 1853, to the opening of 'The Palatial Mart', or 'New Mart', an enterprise of a Corkman named Peter Paul McSwiney, recently arrived in Dublin, and his partner George Delany.[2] In that year Dublin hosted an International Exhibition, inspired by the huge success of the Great Exhibition in London in 1851. These exhibitions were, in themselves, a species of department store, with displays of a wide variety of goods gathered from all over the world. Dublin, which then had a population of only 57,622 families, was crowded with visitors. The exhibition itself was opened on 12 May, and by the time it closed at the end of October it had been visited by nearly a million people – one sixth of the population. Its most distinguished visitors were Queen Victoria and Prince Albert. An important role in the display was played by goods of Irish manufacture.[3] To cater for at least some of the needs of all these strangers the mart managed by McSwiney, Delany & Co. opened its doors to the public for the first time on 28 May. There was perhaps no better moment for opening a new kind of store.

Four large stores already existed. They had first appeared twenty years before, and had grown so large that they had come to be known as 'Monster Marts'. But there was an important distinction between them and the New Mart. The existing four stores had been created by throwing together a series of already existing buildings, as the floor plan of Arnotts in Henry Street (burnt down in 1894) clearly reveals, for the converted rooms of the older buildings still dominated the arrangements. By contrast, the New Mart was purpose built not as a large store, but as a *department store*, and was one of the first, if not the first, of its kind in the world.

The number of floors inside was limited, as in those days before fully safe artificial lighting the interior had to be top-lit from large skylights or windows in the roof. While the buildings on either side of the New Mart (at 23–28 Lower Sackville Street) were still old-fashioned eighteenth-century buildings, the New Mart was five ample floors high, with an arcaded ground floor fronted by a balcony. As originally built, it was eight bays long with a central main entrance. It was a distinguished building, the work of William Caldbeck, a pupil of the eminent architect William Deane Butler.

It was referred to as 'the new Monster House'. *The Builder*, writing about the conditions of Dublin in May 1856, described the 'five leviathan houses of trade' which its columnist 'Quondam' said vastly exceeded anything in London. 'Londoners who have seen Shoolbred's, or Cook's, or Leaf's, would stand amazed [at] the gigantic Irish bazaars', he wrote.[4] At a time when Ireland is all too often seen as labouring under the effects of the Famine, a spirit of enterprise was at large which is often overlooked. It is perhaps most clearly manifest in the New Mart, which exceeded anything in London and, at this date, in Paris, New York or Berlin.

McSwiney's store was itself a new creation. Historians usually date the origins of the modern department store from the opening by Aristide Boucicault (1810–77) of the Magasin du Bon Marché in the rue de Sèvres in 1852, but that firm had existed as a smaller family shop since 1838. Its next rival, the Louvre, was built as a hotel to cater for the Grand Exposition of 1855, and so is later than the Dublin store.

It was not until the 1860s that the Bon Marché took on the attributes of a fully fledged department store, when Aristide Boucicault had the store totally rebuilt to the designs of Eiffel and Boileau in the new technology of steel and glass inspired by Paxton's Great Exhibition buildings in London. This store, which survives, fossilised within the modern Parisian store, was re-opened in 1869.[5] It is to this decade that most of the well-known department stores (such as Whitelys, 'The Universal Provider' in London's Queensway) belong.

McSwiney's Dublin store antedates all this by a very long way, and was on a scale far beyond anything of the day in London. But as it was located in Dublin, its true historical significance has largely been unrecognised by British and European economic historians. The term 'department store' appeared first in print only in 1852, and the scale of this Dublin enterprise suggests that Dublin played a significant, thought long overlooked role, in the early development of this form of retail outlet. The key element in the concept is not sheer *size*, but the notion of *departmental organisation*, in which each department, through its own buyer and accounts, acts as a separate unit, reporting to a central manager.[6] Thus the firm which Denis Guiney took over seems to have a fair claim to being the first purpose-built department store in the world.

The new store was not popular with some. Its critics, the defenders of the smaller, long-established specialist shops which it seemed to be threatening, called it 'the New Monster Store'. But the new phenomenon of the large store was defended in 1851 by no less a person than William Neilson Hancock, Professor of Political Economy at Trinity College, Dublin, who then had a high profile in Irish economics and statistics. The pleas of the Dublin Traders' Association (which spoke for the small traders) he described as little better than 'disguised socialism', that is, an appeal for commu-nity interference in the activities of capitalists. But the controversy raged on. Public meetings were still being organised by the Dublin Traders' Association in 1857, then directed by a draper and former Lord Mayor of Dublin, John Reynolds. A spokesman for the small traders was Isaac Butt, in an early phase of his political career, when as MP for Youghal he was still a Conservative protectionist and Palmerstonian imperialist.[7] (This sort of exchange will be familiar from later, indeed present-day contexts.) Hancock never-theless continued to insist that the monster stores represented both convenience and a greater selection. They turned over the capital invested in them more frequently, and so served the better interests of the greater community.[8]

The department store was, from the point of view of the smaller shops, a severe threat, but it was in keeping with the increasing centralisation of the nineteenth century. The same protests were to be heard a century later when the first suburban supermarkets were introduced from America. The attractiveness of shops selling everything within one establishment was the main feature of both systems.

The department stores, however, also introduced the idea of shopping as pleasure. Customers would go along to such stores, perhaps with vague notions of what they wanted to purchase, but really to take pleasure in the inspection of what was on offer. The department store was a new and novel kind of spectacle; it was, in fact, pure entertainment.

The customers were soon arriving in large numbers to show their approval. They were drawn from the upper eight or ten per cent of the city's population, perhaps some 22,000 out of a total population of 258,361 in 1851. Though the population of the country stood at about 6 million, Dublin was a much smaller place in those days. The customers of McSwiney & Delanys' New Mart were the select folk of the capital. By modern standards the range of goods was limited, and largely aimed at ladies. Men then had their suits made by tailors, while ladies went to dressmakers. The first advertisements of the store were for items in the luxury bracket.

Dublin acted as a magnet to rural people, either moving to live there or for shopping. In 1865 there was another International Exhibition, which brought in another great influx of visitors. During this era the store was identified by the secret police as being a breeding ground for Fenian subversives. Indeed, it was among the drapers' assistants and the small shopkeepers, and not among the farmers and the middle classes, that the republican movement had its strength. One of the staff was arrested in 1866 as a Fenian, though he was later released without being charged.

In 1872 George Delany (who later would be involved in other large firms in Dublin and with the early activities of the Land League) retired from the business. This left McSwiney not only as the sole proprietor of Dublin's first department store but also chairman of what was later claimed to be the first public company in the city – this also a point of some historical significance.

Peter Paul McSwiney is in many ways a typical example of the Catholic middle-class businessman of the nineteenth century, one of those crucial in the transference of economic power from the Protestant merchant class, and with it eventual political power. He was twice elected Lord Mayor of Dublin, and was closely associated with Cardinal Cullen. His main interest, however, lay not in politics but in his department store. The 1860s and 1870s were a time of general prosperity in Ireland. Fashions changed, the crinoline went out, the bustle came in. The fashions of Paris under the Second Empire, especially those of the House of Worth, came to dominate the taste of the fashionable classes. In 1878 McSwiney rebuilt the store, extending the front from eight bays to eleven, absorbing the structure of the adjacent Imperial Hotel into the shop façade. The hotel, however, remained a separate business. But no sooner were these improvements finished than the economic depression of 1879 began, leading to collapse of rents in the west of Ireland and the beginning of the Land War of the 1880s. (The Land League, indeed, was founded at a meeting in the Imperial Hotel on 21 October 1879.) In Dublin many businesses suffered badly, and did not revive in any real way until the end of the 1880s. The loss of revenue was simply a disaster for both the landed and the professional classes, and by extension the expensive stores that served them.

McSwiney was faced with a difficult situation. He recapitalised the store by taking new partners. But age and illness were taking their toll. He too retired, leaving the store, as he thought, in capable hands. (Peter Paul McSwiney died after an operation on 15 August 1884, so bringing to an end a distinct era in the store he founded.) By 1882 the New Mart was bankrupt. As a last resort the name was changed to the Dublin Drapery Warehouse, but even this ploy could not halt the decline. A receiver was called in and the company was wound up. The store was sold to M. J. Clery of Limerick for £32,000 – much less than had been spent simply to renovate it only a few years before, and certainly less than the firm's real value (which had been assessed in February 1882 at £40,000).

II

The new owner established a new company, and in 1883 the firm of Clery & Co. came into legal existence. Michael Clery was a Tipperaryman who had begun his career in Dublin and had subsequently become associated with the firm of Cannocks in Limerick. His family had an obscure but romantic link with Desirée Clary, mistress of Napoleon, who later married Bernadotte and became Queen of Sweden. He had been the editor of the *Nation* for a short period after the arrest of Charles Gavan Duffy. Undoubtedly he knew his trade. Family tradition claimed that he bought the store with a hundred pounds. But though this may have been his stake in the company, the real purchase price was supplied by his friends William Martin Murphy and Murphy's father-in-law, James Fitzgerald Lombard.

The store was certainly bought in Clery's name, but on 6 February 1885 Michael Clery and his brother signed a formal deed of partnership with the two Dublin-based Catholic businessmen, whose money had been made in developing the city's tram system and in the housing developments that went with it, notably in the new township of Drumcondra.

Clery died in 1898. His son Robert took over from him, but he died in 1900. His son died and the last male Clery heir died of influenza in France in 1918. The eldest daughter, however, had married Christopher (later Sir Christopher) Nixon in 1917, and through him the Clery connection was maintained with the firm until 1940.

The paid-up capital of the firm when it was founded was £150,000: £80,000 in preference shares, and £70,000 in ordinary shares, divided unequally among the partners. The new firm was on a sound footing, well supported by financial resources and managerial talent. The 1890s were a period of economic expansion for Dublin. This is the city that appears in the photographs of William Lawrence, a fresh bright city, largely a city of new suburbs reached by the new trams (electrified in 1896) of the Dublin United Tramway Company (founded in 1872 as the Dublin Tramway Company). This concern was owned by William Martin Murphy, who was from Bantry in west Cork. Through his father-in-law, James Fitzgerald Lombard, he had a connection with the Brosna area, for the Lombards came originally from Castleisland. Murphy had begun his professional career at the age of nineteen as a contractor and railway builder and had gone on to develop urban tram systems all over the United Kingdom, and as far away as the Gold Coast (now Ghana) in Africa. Clerys was only a part of many and varied interests. When M. J. Clery died in 1898, the firm was converted into a limited liability company, in which members of the Clery family, Murphy and Lombard were the main shareholders.

The 1890s generally saw a large number of new companies launched in the wake of the business recovery. In all, forty major companies were launched between 1887 and 1897, and total registrations of new companies rose from 50 in the 1880s to 145 in 1897. The quoted capital on the Dublin Stock Exchange went from £7.25 million at the start of the decade to £17.2 million by 1900. It was an era of prosperity, but the prosperity, as was clear to many visitors and reformers in Dublin, was unequally divided.

Clerys shares were not traded. But in 1900, when Robert Clery died and the accountancy firm of Craig Gardner were asked to value the company for probate, they suggested a figure of £222,000. The accountants were initially confident that the company was

4 Clerys 1900 interior

viable and thriving; however, in the annual accounts furnished by
them to the High Court during the minority of the Clery heirs, the
value of the company slowly fell irrespective of profits to £220,413
in January 1914.

In 1902 Clerys bought out the interest of the Lawler family in
the Imperial Hotel, perhaps to take advantage of the expected
surge of visitors to the planned international exhibitions, which
William Martin Murphy was promoting. This was to prove, in
retrospect, one of the landmark events in the years before the
Great War. During the Boer War service of Robert Fitzgerald
Lombard, James's heir, effective control passed into the hands of
the Murphys, now among the richest families in the country. This
was the high point of the old firm, for the 1901 census revealed the
astounding fact that 105 employees actually lived above the shop.
Among its customers was Gertie McDowell, well known to readers
of Joyce's *Ulysses*. Frances Moffatt provides an amusing account of
shopping there in July 1911 and seeing the royal visitors, George V
and Queen Mary, pass by from the balcony.[9]

The connection between W. M. Murphy's various businesses
was commented upon by the contemporary writer Conal O'Riordan
in his novel *Adam of Dublin* (1920). 'That's not the papers only,'
the husband explained, ''tis the thrams and Clerys and the papers
together. Says the *Herald* "Go to Clerys" and the thrams are
waiting there to take them to Clerys, and so to Clerys they go and
spend all their money, and 'tis Murphy has it bad luck to him.'
'The crawling snake,' commented Mrs McFadden; 'not mind you,
but I'd like to be Mrs Murphy.'[10]

These sentiments were uttered about 1912, the year that saw the
first real stirrings of unrest in the city. Economic conditions had
been declining since 1907. The ensuing hardships served only to
increase and so draw attention to the fearful social conditions in the
tenements of Dublin, many of which backed directly on to Clerys
and many of which were actually owned by nationalists.

These tensions exploded in the great lockout of 1913, which was largely organised by James Larkin. The organised employers were led, by chance, by William Martin Murphy. During one demonstration Larkin, disguised as a clergyman, tried to speak to the crowds in the street from the balcony of the Imperial Hotel; but the police quickly arrested him. His detention was followed by a riot outside Clerys in which two men were killed and hundreds injured in police baton charges. It was one of the most appalling events, many thought, in the city's history.

Larkin was jailed. The workers drifted back. But in fact the unions started to organise again and fearing more terrible events, the employers accepted the situation. The riot outside Clerys came to be seen as a turning point in trade union affairs in Ireland.

Political events had been progressing as in the move towards Home Rule. Despite well-organised opposition from Ulster Unionists and English Conservatives, the Home Rule Act was passed in the summer of 1914 and received the royal assent on 18 September. But it was suspended with the outbreak of European war in the autumn – a war that was to mark the real end of the Victorian era in which Clerys had been created. It was not perhaps until the middle of 1915 that Europeans realised that their continent had entered on a war that was to change everything. In Ireland too the consequences would be enormous. Yet the full extent to which life would change did not become apparent until 1919.

The original Clerys (the building of 1853) was burnt down in 1916 during the Easter Rising. As soon as peace was restored it was rebuilt, on a far grander scale. William Martin Murphy died in June 1919, during the planning period, so it was left to his son, Dr W. Lombard Murphy, to complete the great task of rebuilding Clerys, making it once more a landmark of what would now be officially called O'Connell Street. It was intended to bring Dublin the latest in shopping facilities, and the architectural firm of

Ashlin & Coleman based their design on the new Selfridges in London, thought of then as the last word in department store design. Clerys was reopened on 9 August 1922, soon after the city-centre fighting at the outbreak of the Civil War, in which Guiney lost his little store in Talbot Street, came to an end.

Murphy's sons, who had taken over from him, did not want to maintain all his interests. Dr Lombard Murphy was more interested in the newspapers in Abbey Street, though he remained chairman of Clerys. His brother Christopher was manager of the shop, but though he had been groomed for the post, having served time in Derry & Toms in London, the Dublin store proved too much for him. He was not able to reverse the losses accumulated in the years of the Troubles.

In 1923 Christopher Murphy resigned, and John McGuire and his son Edward became managing director and assistant manager of Clerys. Both were accomplished businessmen and astute managers. John McGuire had an exceptional contract which gave him total control. He was also to have a special commission. Soon he turned the store around and was earning, aside from his salary, a very large commission of £47,798 over the decade from 1923.

The store prospered and retained its leading position. But by 1930 times had become difficult again. The full impact of the depression was delayed in Ireland until 1932, largely because as an agricultural country it was less affected by the collapse of cereal prices. However, in spite of the economic downturn, at Clerys the profits and commission continued to mount. In 1933 the board decided to bring McGuire's contract, which had six years to run, to an end. His closure of the religious goods department, which had been overstocked with pious gewgaws for the Eucharistic Congress in 1932, was merely a *casus belli*. The Murphys wanted a dividend at last. Before the dividend could be paid McGuire claimed he should receive his unpaid commission, which was part of his legal remuneration. The board refused to pay it and dismissed him. He then sued. In the end it was ruled that the board had been acting *ultra vires* by making the contract in the first place. The board won their case through their own incompetence, which says a great deal about the heirs of those giants Murphy and Lombard. The McGuires moved on to greater things in Brown Thomas.

The board now appointed an internal manger, who proved a disaster. Faced with excess stock, he ordered buyers to cut back, rather than sell more at cheaper prices and create cash flow. As trade conditions worsened during the 'Economic War' Clerys declined. Sir Christopher Nixon, a connection of the original Clery, became chairman in 1931, replacing Dr Lombard Murphy, and in 1938 he took over as managing director. His career had been in the British army, though he had had a couple of years in business management in London. And it was he, rather than members of the Murphy family, who had adroitly washed their hands of a failure, who had to face the difficult years of the late 1930s. They proved too much for him. Sales and profits fell. By 1940 the profit had sunk to a net return of £1,636.

III

Disaster faced the firm by the end of 1939. Early in 1940 its creditors began to exert real pressure. The leading claim was one by Equity and Law Life Assurance for a 1936 loan of £200,000. The staff, anxious for their future, made an offer to accept a cut in wages, but this was no solution for a firm losing business. A new, more easily managed shop was sought by the board. But in vain. The problem was not with the staff costs, or even with the building; it lay entirely at the management style of Sir Christopher Nixon.

In 1940 a receiver was brought in. He was Eustace Shott of the accountants Craig Gardner. As this firm had long been Clerys' accountants, and as Shott was known to all and well liked, the board saw him in the light of an ally in the present difficulties. But as is the way with troubled firms, Shott's first duty was not to the board, but to the debenture-holders and the creditors. To their horror, the board found he was intent on disposing of the company's assets and discharging the debenture for the benefit of Equity and Law Life Assurance. He closed the store and dismissed the staff.

Now, of course, he was faced, in the early days of the wartime Emergency, with the problem of finding a buyer. Certainly no British firm came forward, even though there were widespread fears in Dublin of a foreign, or possibly Jewish, takeover. (This is a curious instance of the anti-Semitism that lurks just below the social surface in Ireland.) Apart from the accumulated debts, Clerys was trading at a loss and would find it hard to import goods in wartime. Shott set up a committee of the trade creditors to advise him, an unusual step in those days. Potential buyers were sounded out in Dublin, but it was felt that the stock was too old and too highly valued on the books.

Eventually early in November 1940 Shott approached Denis Guiney, who was clearly trading very profitably in nearby Talbot Street to see if he would be interested in taking over Clerys. Though he might rival Clerys in turnover, the larger store would be a move into a new area of business presentation. It could be an enormous risk.

Guiney walked over the premises with Shott, and a mere two days later he made an offer to buy Clerys as a going concern for £225,000. He had valued the store by eye rather than by any arithmetical assessment. But he rightly insisted on an immediate decision, as keeping the shop closed for any long period would make reopening more difficult. It was essential, he felt, to take advantage of the approaching Christmas season, the most important sales period of the year for any business of this kind. He demanded an answer by 15 November 1940.

Shott called the creditors together. They accepted what had now become a slightly higher offer from Guiney, giving them all a shilling in the pound. In the event, this money went to the staff, many of whom had deposited their life savings with Clerys and had lost them. Denis Guiney paid over a deposit of £20,000 and took over the store at once. The remainder of the money he raised himself from the Munster and Leinster Bank.

The former board was horrified by these developments. One cannot but think that on the part of Sir Christopher Nixon and his board there was an element of snobbery: their genteel family firm was being sold off to some *arriviste* son of a Kerry farmer. At the end of November 1940 they took action against Shott and Guiney in the High Court to have the sale set aside. The matter came to a hearing in the summer of 1941. The board's case was that the price offered was insufficient, that the assets should have been sold separately to realise a higher price, that the receiver had hurried the sale, thus preventing them from making arrangements with the bankers, and that the final price was fixed to cover debenture debts and expenses, and not the true value of the stock.

In his judgement Mr Justice Gavan Duffy (a son of the nineteenth-century patriot Sir Charles Gavan Duffy) decided in favour of Shott and Guiney. He failed to see any merit at all in the idea of Clerys having a value beyond the value which the market placed upon the firm. Sir Christopher had talked in court of Clerys being 'a gold mine sold at scrap-metal prices'. But Sir Christopher had failed to make a profit from this 'gold mine', and no other buyer had offered more than Guiney. 'Yet such a witness would have been of far more practical value than the most glowing description of the finest site in the capital', Gavan Duffy commented.

He accepted that Guiney's methods in the matter of assessing the company 'were unorthodox as they were direct. He consulted no valuer, brought in no accountant, required no special stock-taking . . . he did not trouble to examine the Company's accounts.' But he had made an offer, and no one else had. In this case, at least, market values – the watchword of capitalism – ruled.

So the sale of an important part of the William Martin Murphy empire to Denis Guiney was confirmed, and Clerys entered upon a new era of its long history. Guiney completed the purchase with a cheque for £230,000 to Shott from his new company on 10 September 1941. 'Our Dinny', as Dubliners saw it, had made a cute deal, and that inevitably this won the admiration of a nation descended from Celtic horse-traders, Viking pirates and Norman robber barons.

Soon after taking over Clerys Guiney applied for a licence to sell intoxicating liquor for consumption on the premises. It was refused. Eventually Denis Guiney got his liquor licence, and also one for dancing, but only after new legislation was passed by the Oireachtas some years later.[11] The Beehive, as the bar was called, became his own special place of resort in the afternoons.

Denis Guiney, the new owner of Clerys, was a social type in contrast to Sir John Arnott, the founder of Arnotts, or to Peter Paul McSwiney, James Fitzgerald Lombard and William Martin Murphy. He represented a shift in economic power away from the middle classes, both Protestant and Catholic, towards the Catholic lower middle class and upper working class – towards, in fact, the typical Fianna Fáil voter.

In buying Clerys, Denis Guiney brought together two very different styles of marketing. He had been trained in the small-store rural system, and this was what he applied, more or less, in Talbot Street. Now in buying up a department store, he moved into the very different area of the retailing world, with a very different approach to marketing, which had evolved since the middle of the nineteenth century. However, he would apply here much that he had found successful in his earlier career, creating, in the later part of his life, a unique institution in the life of Dublin city.

CHAPTER 5

The Proprietor of Clerys, 1940-9[1]

I

Long before nine o'clock on 29 November 1940 crowds had gathered outside Clerys on the wide pavement on O'Connell Street. The milling numbers were an extraordinary sight. Across the great plate glass windows banners announced in huge letters 'Grand Opening Sale', 'Complete Clearance of Stocks', 'Xmas Stocks at Bargain Prices'.

The capital's historic street had not seen such a crowd for years. With Christmas only weeks away, the lure of the real bargains to be had, of nice presents for next to nothing was too good to be missed. Moreover, this was perhaps a last chance to pick up pre-war goods as the shadow of war moved closer. Extra staff had to be brought to deal with the rush. In the shoe department, for instance, where there were usually a mere four assistants, twenty were serving that morning.

For Dubliners this was no ordinary sale. This was a Denis Guiney sale – and the city had long known what good value that meant. Since the 1920s his own shop in Talbot Street had been famous for its wonderful bargains. In his sales goods would be slashed to unbelievably low prices, giving the best value for money in Ireland – anywhere in the world, some enthusiasts claimed.

5 Crowds outside Clerys at reopening sale, November 1940

This sale was special in another way too. Only weeks before a rumour had spread that Clerys, the city's largest department store by far, was doomed. The long dreaded European war had come after the long difficult years of the 1930s, in Ireland marked not only by the effects of the worldwide depression but also by the 'Economic War' with the United Kingdom. These conditions had proved too much for the old management of Clerys. Now the store had risen from the ashes. The first day's takings were £14,260. In the first week after the reopening under the new management Clerys did £54,000 worth of business, almost certainly a record in Irish retailing.

The following year, in August 1941, Denis Guiney established a new company to run the store, Clery & Co. (1941) Ltd., capitalised at £250,000. This is the present company that still owns the store.

It was kept distinct and separate from his original firm in Talbot Street. Two years before his death Guiney laconically recalled the most momentous event of his career:

> I couldn't do any more trade in Talbot Street. I looked around for another store, and so, in 1940 I bought out Clerys lock, stock and barrel. I won't tell you what price I paid for it: that's top secret to this day . . . I couldn't get enough work in those days and I enjoyed every second of it. I now had the best stand in Ireland for a shop and getting people in was easy after that. Give them the bargains and the quality, and you can't lose.

An old man's memory of his greatest coup here takes on, in hindsight, the aura of casual necessity. But the plain fact was that Denis Guiney faced an immense challenge. As usual, he rose to meet it.

The early days, with the sale and other pressures, were difficult and chaotic. The story is told of one sharp operator who took advantage of the muddle by boldly walking into the shop and getting hold of a sales book. For a week before he was found out he happily pocketed the money from his sales, reaping a tidy profit for himself during that hectic time. The old Clerys staff assumed he was one of the new staff brought in from Talbot Street to help out, while the Talbot Street people assumed he was from Clerys.

The general interest aroused by the legal action against himself and Shott, which was heard early in July 1941, and a long interview published the following January in the new and highly regarded literary journal, *The Bell*, edited by Sean O'Faolain, gave a vivid impression of the man quite beyond the usual journalism of the day.

Denis Guiney was not associated much with matters of literary culture. But at the end of July 1941 he granted space in Clerys to the F. R. Higgins Memorial Fund to display some sixteen canvases by leading Irish artists – one of which was left blank for Leo Whelan to paint to order a portrait for the winner of a lottery for the pictures. The poet, one of the most promising of the post-Yeatsian generation, had died suddenly at a young age in January, and the memorial was to take the form of a monument by sculptor Jerome Connor in the graveyard at Laracor where Higgins was buried. It was never erected.

Later that year, on 11 September 1941, Guiney even appeared on stage. He took part in an interview with Roy Irving, a popular feature of 'Hullabaloo No. 9', the early evening variety stage show at the Theatre Royal, put on between screenings of René Clair's film *The Flame of New Orleans*, starring the smouldering Marlene Dietrich. In those days before TV interviews became ubiquitous this was a very rare opportunity for a public figure to speak about his life before a large audience, Dublin in those days having one of the largest cinema-going populations in the world.

Guiney told Irving that the main qualification for success in business was to give the best service to customers. A good bargain to the customer was a good bargain for the businessman. The most important thing was to give good value for money, and a man should know his particular line of trade thoroughly and always have the money to buy well. In business one had always to be going forward, or the reverse was likely to happen. He had taken over a big new business in Clerys, but by carrying out his established policy of giving the public what they wanted, he felt reasonably confident of making it a success. The principal problem of the present time was to obtain sufficient goods of sufficient variety, but he was more concerned about post-war difficulties. The war, however, would run for another four years.[2]

These interviews meant that Denis Guiney began his time at Clerys very much in the public eye. This was not where he wanted to be. He preferred to get on with the job in hand. The reopening sale was only a preliminary to a transformation of the whole store.

All looked set fair, commented *Irish Industry*, 'provided Mr Guiney gets a fair deal from the Trade Unions. They are the unknown quantities in the whole equation.'[3] Almost at once trouble arose over the introduction of more up-to-date methods into the Accounts Department in Clerys, which led to a brief strike. The unions were not the only source of criticism for some practices in Irish business. Dr Lucey, the outspoken Catholic Bishop of Cork and Ross, was among those who found the mere pursuit of profit objectionable. But at this time others were also trying to put into action, through social studies groups, some of the principles of society expounded by the Church.[4]

Neither independence in 1922 nor the advent to power of Fianna Fáil in 1932 saw much amelioration of the social and economic conditions for many Irish people – 43 per cent of whom still lived on the land, and were badly affected by the Economic War that de Valera initiated against the United Kingdom over the payment of the annuities due under the old Land Act.

In these decades of economic difficulty, many Catholic intellectuals were interested in social study groups and in efforts to apply to Ireland such progressive papal teachings as *Rerum Novarum*, which had been promulgated as far back as 1891, and reiterated by *Quadragesimo Anno* in 1931. Others, among them Denis Guiney, took more immediate practical measures. Guiney was not a member of such an organisation as the Knights of St Columbanus, as many middle-class Catholics were. His Catholic associations were with the board of Jervis Street Hospital on which he served for many years, the night shelter for men in Back Lane and the St Vincent de Paul Society.

He was also well known for his own kindness and private acts of charity. When he died one Catholic newspaper said he 'had a genius for helping in a quiet, unostentatious way, but with a generosity that was full and satisfying'.[5]

Thousands of stories were told about this. A Dublin mother had a daughter employed in Clerys who left to enter a convent. Being in poor circumstances, she asked Guiney if he would employ in her place a younger daughter. He agreed. Could he fit her out also? – at this time all the women employed in Clerys wore a black uniform dress with a white cotton collar. 'What size is she?' The two girls were the same size, the mother said. 'There wasn't much of her in it', Guiney remarked. When the new girl reported for work on the following Monday a complete outfit was ready for her.

The closure of the religious department had been one of the mistakes with which Ned McGuire had been charged. Guiney restored the clerical tailoring department, as well as the clerical outfitting and the church furnishings. The custom of the clergy had always been important to Clerys, and before that to McSwiney & Delany. William Martin Murphy, for instance, had been the proprietor of the *Irish Catholic*, in those days a vigorous anti-Parnellite paper. There was a clerical perception that the other great department stores in Dublin were 'Protestant' or, worse still, 'Masonic' firms. With a rising number of clerical students and a large population of priests and nuns, Guiney knew a valuable niche market when he saw it. But it ought to be said that this was by definition a conservative market. Embracing the needs of the Church, by supplying everything from soutanes to Stations of the Cross, was an indication that the firm might fail in due time to respond to more rapidly changing lay demands in the future.

This was only one change of many. 'I rebuilt the restaurant, bars and ballroom. I spent £83,000 in altering the ballroom alone, and £250,000 in all', Guiney recalled again in 1965. (This appears to refer to the purchase price, even though he once said he wouldn't tell anyone what he had paid for Clerys.) 'There are dances here seven nights a week, and there is a full-time orchestra employed. I never danced in my life. Couldn't, even if you paid me!' His new

6 Guiney's store still suited the clergy

and elegant Art Deco ballroom was for many young Dubliners in the 1940s and 1950s their very own 'Ballroom of Romance', a social feature now quite alien to a generation reared on discos. Clerys was an immensely popular venue, but then a weekly dance date was an important part of the life of most young people. They went to the halls in those days more for the dancing and the opportunity to meet other young people than for the drink and the crack. Sackville Place would be crammed with unlocked bicycles on dance nights – in a Dublin free of cars and thieves. The bands – for this was the era of the big bands – were also an attraction. Jack Hilton's was only one of the famous groups that were booked.

To open all these new ventures required a drinks licence as well as a dance licence. At first Denis Guiney was refused one, or at least his new company was. Eventually the Intoxicating Liquor Act of 1943, which some Dubliners saw as being specially introduced by the Fianna Fáil government for the benefit of Denis Guiney, opened up a new opportunity for him to circumvent the decision of the district justice at the original hearing. So he got what he wanted: a bar licence. The original refusal seems odd indeed, for the building had been an hotel and licensed premises under other earlier managements; but, of course, Denis Guiney's was a totally new company in the eyes of the law.

The ballroom and the restaurants and the Beehive Bar were all opened by 1944. By then the war was coming to an end. In 1942 the government had introduced rationing and price controls on clothing as an Emergency measure. A great march of both employees and employers in the drapery trade was held in 1942. Denis Guiney found himself marching with Edward McGuire then of Brown Thomas, and Ronald Nesbitt of Arnotts, representing the Drapers' Chamber of Commerce (founded in 1932), in which he had always been active. They walked from Parnell Square along a traditional protest route to Leinster House in Kildare Street.

The drapery trade found its margins reduced by the government to 25 per cent for retail and 15 per cent for wholesale. This turned out to benefit trade by making some goods more attractive. Wages were in turn controlled by the Wages Standstill Order of May 1941. Controls too were introduced on the amount of fabric that went into made-up garments, dresses became simpler and hems narrower. In 1941 the Merchant Drapers' Association was liquidated: its name alone was redolent of an old-fashioned approach. It was replaced, under the Trade Union Act of 1941, by the Federated Union of Employers.[6]

The war made life hard for traders in Dublin, but it is said that, even at the height of the war, such was the sheer volume of Denis Guiney's trade, that he had no difficulty finding space on the boats from England. (Odd things happened in those days. From Belgium just after the war, he brought a cargo of chocolates, a luxury unheard of for many years. But he could not sell it, for it was not the mild milk chocolate the Irish preferred, but dark, bitter continental chocolate. He had to burn the lot unsold.)

Having acquired Clerys, Guiney rapidly restored its trading position. But he had also to maintain the turnover of his original store. Here he depended on the advertising skills of his friend P. L. McEvoy. In the middle of May 1941 they began publishing *Guiney's News*, which continued until August 1947. They also published in 1945 an eighty-page book for children, called *Guiney's Story Book, with pictures for painting* – though this experiment was not repeated.[7] There was also a series of childrens' classics.

Advertising in Ireland was then a fairly low-key affair, rather old-fashioned in its approaches. These novel ideas were very American, and are an indication of the 'give it a try' attitude of Denis Guiney. They were intended to keep the public aware of the Talbot Street shop and its bargains, but the idea of the book for children was a bold stroke, depending for its appeal on the better instincts of most Irish mothers.

The Emergency restrictions on newsprint, which was imported, meant that the regular newspapers were not able to carry their usual level of advertising. *Guiney's News* was started to provide Guiney with a vehicle of his own to promote not only the Talbot Street store, but also Clerys. But the paper was very much a general publication, for it carried beauty tips, household advice, historical pieces, quizzes, and other kinds of items, some original, some syndicated. It contained many curious things.

There was, for instance, a sponsored 'Question Time' at the Carlton Cinema, with Mr Guiney presenting the prizes. The lending library at Clerys, very much a middle-class affair, was – so it was claimed – under the personal supervision of Mr Guiney, and the paper began to carry notices of new books from March 1944.

'Bare your legs', screamed a headline. But the paper suggested more than that. Ireland was then a fairly prudish country, yet a series on the health benefits of sunbathing recommended a process of partial exposure to expose the body piece by piece until it was completely exposed. Without the claimed medical benefits, it is hard to think nude sunbathing would have been commended in 1940s Ireland. But that such a suggestion could be made at all is an interesting comment on the social attitudes of some Dubliners.

The paper eschewed current events, the war passing almost entirely without reference until the end of August 1943. At the time of the general elections (two coming quickly upon each other in June 1943 and May 1944) the duty to vote was emphasised in an article which commented on the dangers of inappropriate, even anti-democratic, persons having been elected elsewhere. However, it concluded, 'There is not much danger of candidates being elected in Ireland likely to aid and abet measures contrary to religion or morality.' But there was an unusual development with the entry of America into the war: 'Fashions from Hollywood' and a column of film notes appeared. McEvoy at the same time was busy promoting an annual devoted to film stars, entitled *The Screen Album*.

A cartoon by Alec Warner, a well-known cartoonist of the day, showed Batemanesque caricature of a little man causing havoc and panic in Clerys. He is shown asking Mr Guiney: 'How's Business?' The answer was, of course, 'Thriving.' Thriving, indeed, to such an extent that in January 1946 Guiney had been approached by a firm acting for a London group, rumoured then to be the flour and film corporation J. Arthur Rank, interested in buying the store – this may well have been a part of that short-term flight of capital from the Labour Party's socialist Britain into the Irish Free State where prices were then so very much cheaper and the 'red' threat non-existent. However, Guiney, who was only just getting into his stride at Clerys, and with what seemed like good post-war prospects in the offing, was not interested. It is said that when Rank himself heard the price that might be asked, he said it would be cheaper to make another *Hamlet*, a film version of which directed by Laurence Olivier was taking up much of his time and money in the immediate post-war years.

On 7 May 1946 the silver jubilee of the opening of Guineys was celebrated by the staff with a dinner dance at which a sliver presentation was made to Mr and Mrs Guiney, not only by those who worked in Talbot Street, but also those who had transferred to Clerys. This touching act of homage was a reflection of the benefits they all felt. That year sales rose to £2.7 million, even though the profits were only £16,000, a mere ½ per cent. Denis Guiney's toast to 'Ireland' cannot have been as heartily welcomed as was the toast to 'Denis Guiney' by the president of the Federation of Irish Manufacturers and the vice-president of the Drapers' Chamber of Commerce. They well knew the value of Denis Guiney to Irish trade.

The company was undoubtedly prospering. Indeed it was at this time that Denis bought out the leases on the promises he occupied. Dubliners may have thought he used Guiney's to buy Clerys; in

7 Denis Guiney and his wife Mary in the 1940s

reality he used the credit of Clerys to buy Guiney's. In 1947 the
new company purchased the Talbot Street Furnishing Company,
a shop across the road from the original store, near the junction
with Amiens Street, where many similar, though smaller, firms
were grouped. The new shop soon had the distinction recorded on
its notepaper of being under the personal direction of Mr Denis
Guiney, for Dubliners a sure guarantee of quality at the right price.

Peace in Europe had not brought an end to rationing. Indeed, in Ireland conditions in the late 1940s and early 1950s were worse than during the Emergency. The cost-of-living index peaked in 1947 at 319 points (from 173 points in August 1939). The years of economic deprivation had also begun to fray tempers. There was a National Teachers' strike in 1946 lasting eight months, a strike of bus and tram workers in 1947, the year bread and flour were rationed for the first time in Ireland. Clerys itself was closed in July by a strike.

The immediate cause of this strike was the transfer of an employee from the lucrative carpets department to one with a lower commission. This was deemed unfair. Guiney refused to worry. He took himself and his wife off as usual for their annual holiday in Ballybunion in Kerry, leaving the staff to their own devices. However, the rumour reached him that a buyout was being organised by some of the senior staff – possibly with the connivance of the Munster and Leinster Bank, which still held a large section of shares – so he came hurrying back to the city. The strike was quickly settled and a monster sale immediately announced.

The strike seems to have had little effect, for the annual profit (as recorded in January 1948) was £76,000 on sales of £2.7 million, making a net profit of 2.8 per cent. This position had been achieved by a £1m loan to cover restocking, but the subsequent sales meant that the loan was quickly repaid, and Clerys closed the decade once again in a healthy, indeed vigorous position. It was to be hoped that the 1950s would be even better.

Guiney had created a 'ballroom of romance' encouraging the young to associate on Clerys premises, to buy a Clerys engagement ring, marry in Clerys dress, buy their new household goods from Clerys, their children's clothes and Christmas presents from Clerys, and so on. In a country where dance halls had been the subject of controversy in the early 1930s, and where notoriously marriage was often long avoided, this was progressive. His full-page advertisements represented the possibilities of a new abundance. The typical Irish working-class dwelling, with its drab and often bare interior and its strictly functional kitchen, could be decorated and curtained, could be transformed into a comfortable home. Mr de Valera, himself housed in a large mansion in a respectable suburb, and with his children educated for the professions, might speak of the ideal of 'frugal comfort': Denis Guiney sold lace curtains and soft cushions.

In this sense the effect of Denis Guiney was revolutionary. Others might speak of preserving Irish culture, and yet others of a workers' paradise. What Guiney offered was the chance for everyone to be middle class. He catered for the aspirations of people, giving them what they wanted, not what it was said they should have. He offered the clerk the opportunity of dressing as well as his boss, his wife the opportunity of making her house as comfortable as the boss's own. His great achievement was to change the material and social culture directly, to confront how people lived with dreams of how they might live. He is thus one of the essential creators of the character of modern Ireland as a consumer society ruled by market forces. From the cradle to the grave, by way of first Holy Communion and Confirmation, Clerys catered for the national needs, material and spiritual.

II

Two contrasting enterprises took up much of Guiney's time in the years after the war, continuing on into later decades. After the war he was one of the first to realise the potential of Irish exports. He established a company called Beleir, a Belgo-Irish enterprise, which had offices in both Dublin and Brussels. The notion was to export Irish agricultural produce and to import continental farm

machinery, fertilisers and other goods. The Belgian chocolates mentioned above were one example. A Beleir shop retailing
imported fancy glassware was opened at 16 Talbot Street – previously occupied by a Guiney nephew as an outfitters – directly
opposite Guiney's own store. Beleir continued to trade from offices
in Lower Baggot Street until nearly the end of the 1950s, before
being formally dissolved in 1961. But among Denis Guiney's
various enterprises Beleir cannot be accounted a success. He was
moving out of the retail area he knew intimately, and though there
were only about a dozen or so firms who acted as importers and
exporters in this way (rather than as agents), the goods imported
could not compete.

In all things he remained a loyal son of Kerry, supporting the
Kerrymen's Association and the GAA. He also took his annual
holiday in Kerry at Ballybunion, staying in the Castle Hotel. From
the late 1940s, when the town began to blossom as a holiday resort,
the new Irish wealthy such as Denis Guiney began to flock there. The
Castle Hotel was the place to be, with 'legal types and clergy' making up the bulk of the visitors. The main street was so packed with
priests in their black suits that local people nicknamed it the Vatican.
'The hotel had a magnificent ballroom, women wore beautiful frocks
and locals weren't allowed in', recalled a local resident recently.

A strictly non-commercial Kerry venture in which Guiney
became involved in these years was the Derrynane Trust, whose
purpose was to save and preserve for the nation Daniel
O'Connell's former home at Derrynane Abbey near Caherdaniel,
County Kerry. Guiney served as chairman of the Trust from its
establishment in 1946 to 1964. Its aim was to mark the centenary of
O'Connell's death in May 1847 by restoring his ancestral mansion.
The house and a small amount of land were passed by the family to
the Trust in 1946, and in an appeal published from Clerys, over the
signatures of Denis Guiney and the Lord Mayor of Dublin, John

McCann, TD, funds were sought. The committee had a council of patronage under Cardinal D'Alton, the Catholic Primate, and composed of cardinals and archbishops around the world. The aim was twofold: to save the abbey from the decay then threatening it, and to restore it as a shrine not only to the patriot, but 'to leave it as a perpetual shrine for the Most Blessed Sacrament reserved there by special Papal Privilege, in recognition of O'Connell's priceless services to humanity'.[8] This ambition was quite in keeping with the publicly pietistic tone of the national discourse in those days as mediated by those sensitive souls, the paid journalists of the national newspapers.

Denis Guiney, actively supported by his wife, spoke at a public meeting in the Dublin Mansion House, on 15 May 1947, presided over by Archbishop McQuaid, and used his influence to gather support and money for the cause of the Save Derrynane Committee.[9] He had started the fund rolling by subscribing 1,000 guineas, as had the National Bank, 'the Liberator's Bank', founded by O'Connell in 1834. (The guineas, the preferred style of payment to senior professionals, were a nice touch of class distinction.)

The committee became the Derrynane Trust in 1948, taking over the house from the Liberator's great-great-grandson, the historian Professor Maurice D. O'Connell. Over the next eighteen years the Trust spent some £12,000 on the house, £5,000 of which came by way of grants from the government. But they could not raise enough money to finish the task. Public attitudes towards O'Connell were ambivalent: while to some he was the great patriot who had won Catholic Emancipation, to others he was an abject royalist who opposed physical-force nationalism, a landed gentleman who evicted his tenants in times of hardship. His grandson about the time of the rise of Sinn Féin had written eloquently as a Catholic Unionist against Home Rule. In an era of revived republican enthusiasm, many regarded him and his grandfather as little better than traitors. Accordingly, the fund languished. No more than £4,800 – less than a pound a day over the long-drawn-out years – was collected. One of Kerry's great heroes, it seems O'Connell lacked universal appeal.

The committee raised enough to restore the chapel and to open a small museum, but had difficulties in keeping up the house, the rooms of which were filled with sentimental – 'if hideously Victorian' – relics of the Liberator. But the work of the Trust was characterised in 1962 as 'ill-advised restorations'. Eventually, in December 1963, embarrassed by such remarks from influential sources on the state of Derrynane, the committee under Guiney appealed again to the government, which finally decided to take the place over, and the house was handed from the Trust to the state in December 1964, the deeds being passed in February 1965 to Seán Lemass by Denis Guiney at celebratory event in Clerys.

The Office of Public Works set about repairs to the fabric and interiors which were completed in 1967. The original mansion, which formed the main part of the house, 'a wanly appealing Georgian house' dating from the 1750s – said to have been 'the first slated house in south Kerry' – had indeed decayed through long years of neglect beyond retrieval while in the hands of the Derrynane Trust, and had to be demolished, leaving the Victorian additions made by O'Connell himself.[10]

The house was re-opened in August 1967. In a dedication speech President de Valera admitted that his generation had misjudged O'Connell, that the Liberator had had to do what he could in the circumstances of his own time. A counter view was published by Guiney's old friend Gerald Boland who admitted the President's speech had annoyed him and who in a letter to the press attacked O'Connell and the O'Connell family from the Republican point of view. This led to a lively public correspondence with many defending O'Connell and more extreme Republicans attacking Boland for his harsh treatment of the IRA when he was Minister of Justice in the 1940s. Guiney was widely admired and thanked for what he had done, both in Kerry and elsewhere, but even a gesture towards preserving the heritage of Kerry and of Ireland could, he found, be mired in the controversies of modern politics.

The Derrynane Trust, for all Guiney's work and the admiring comments from the Kerrymen's Association and others, had been a failure, along with Beleir, one of Denis Guiney's very few. He had attached his name to a national cause, but the talented salesman had found few to buy into it. He would never do anything like it again.

In Dublin, however, things still went well for the Guineys. Around the city itself the tide of change was flowing. Trams, for instance, had been of much importance to the city and, let us not forget, to Clerys since their introduction in 1872. They enabled the people of the suburbs to reach the city centre. Now buses and the increasingly common private cars had overtaken them. These were the days when many of the Clerys staff actually went home for their dinners at midday – one of them as far as Dalkey.

For many Dubliners an era ended when the last tram left Nelson's Pillar outside Clerys for Dalkey on 10 July 1949, witnessed by a huge and sentimental crowd outside Clerys. The new green buses, while modern and up-to-date, lacked the appeal of the old trams. With their going Dublin lost a little of its old-fashioned Victorian charm. Some suspected it might even be on the way to becoming a modern city.

CHAPTER 6

Through Leaner Years, 1950-9

For Clerys the 1950s was a decade of growth after a time of great difficulty during the extended Emergency which only ended effectively in 1948. The 1950s opened with a bank strike which lasted from December 1950 through the middle of February 1951. In the prevailing atmosphere of post-war gloom, and the impending world threatening outbreak of the Korean War, it was not an auspicious beginning to the new decade.

Unemployment and emigration remained high, as general indicators of economic and social malaise. Nevertheless, Clerys was able to maintain Denis Guiney's well-tried policies of quality goods at cheap prices. This made Clerys a very attractive shopping place in the period.

The autumn season of 1951, for instance, had bargains gathered after weeks of selection from the fashion houses of Ireland, Britain and France. The variety on offer was very great because of Clerys' buying policy. In the full-page advertisements which were a feature of the period women's clothes predominated, along with those for girls and children. While the most expensive ladies' overcoat was an all-wool check at 14 guineas, there were others priced down to 7 guineas (present-day values would be about €100 to €190). 'A real smart coat for autumn' was described as 'being carried out in fine wool whipcord material. It is cut on classical lines with a fly-away collar, wide reveres, double breasted, slit pockets, broad panel effect gathered bodice in back with half-belt and vented pleat.'

Ladies blouses, that handy index of changing prices, were 32s 6d. But it was the hats that really set the period tone: dainty little objects with small veils and mock feathers 'a pleasantly bewildering variety' from 25s 11d to 4½ guineas. Also on offer was fashion's most modern trend: 'NYLON LINGERIE ALONG WITH CORSETS TO SUIT THE NEW FASHIONS '.

Clerys managed astutely to offer both up-to-date clothes and those that combined features appealing to a largely conservative market. Those lingerie ads emphasised snug stylishness rather than anything of direct sexual allure. For Ireland, as a whole, was not so much fashion-conscious as value-orientated in those bleak days of the early 1950s.

In the autumn of 1952 the government introduced a restrictive practices bill. This was opposed by many businessmen who held a meeting on the matter in Dublin on 21 October. The tone of the speeches was very defensive. One speaker from the Electrical Trades Association said it was a dangerous and dictatorial measure which 'could lead to a socialist form of state'. That kind of talk touched one nerve in the body public. Denis Guiney pricked another. He said that those at the meeting and the government knew well that these restrictive practices were going one.

The Minister knows the names and addresses of these firms — I was one of those people who supplied them. Not alone is there a monopoly made for them here, but they also want to make money for their pals and associates of some particular organization. I don't believe the Minister will believe that you are serious if you send in this resolution.

This state was built up by and for the Irish people, but when a lot of foreigners come into it and get a monopoly in certain trades, only members of the so-called Masonic Order can get it. A Catholic firm

STOCKINGS

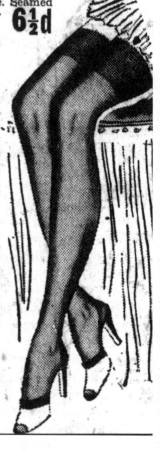

Ladies' Art. Silk 300 needle hose. Seamed backs. Good range of shades. Every pair perfect. Worth 10½d. Sale price **6½d**

Ladies' plaited Silk Hose. Ideal for hard wear. Summer Sale price **6½d**

Clearing line of good heavy quality Art. Silk Hose. Available in the new sun tan shades. Reduced for the Sale from 1/11 to **8½d**

A marvellous offer of Ladies' pure silk Hose. Three shades only. Genuine price 1/11. Sale Price **1/-**

A good range of Ladies' heavy Silk Hose. In various shades. Also black and dull mixtures. Perfect goods. Per pair **1/-**

Ladies' Pure Silk Hose. With or without contrasting heels. Every pair perfect. Selling elsewhere at 1/11 and 2/6 per pair. Guineys Sale price **1/6½**

Marvellous value in Ladies' fully fashioned Bemberg Hose. Season's newest shades. Per pair **1/11½**

Ladies' Pure Silk Crepe Hose. Newest shades. Per pair **2/6**
Also large variety of Ankle Socks at 8½d., White 10½d., 1/3½, and 1/6½.

8 The younger woman was now an important customer

won't get it. That is what is happening in this country and it will have
to be stopped. The Irish people will stop it if the Minister does not.[1]

This was one of the very few times that Denis Guiney made
what could be called an overtly political speech. Here his
vocabulary echoes that of the most conservative elements in
contemporary Irish society. Many in the commercial classes of
Dublin were obsessed with fears of Socialist agitation and
Masonic influence, even though the Left had little real influence
on Irish affairs and Freemasonry had been in decline since the mid-
1920s. Indeed the influence of the Knights of St Columbanus,
which many Catholic businessmen and civil servants were members
of, was seen by many as a reaction to these fears, for that association
dated its rise to prominence from about the same period. However,
it would only be with the creation of a more vigorous Irish economy
under Seán Lemass after 1960, in which enterprises passed not
from Protestant to Catholic hands but on into international owner-
ship, that these fears would, to some extent, fade away. But before
then Ireland had to pass through the slough of the 1950s.

An effort to raise the spirits of the country and to attract visitors
was the creation of the annual Tóstal event, an 'Ireland at home'
extravaganza. It was first held in 1953, when its opening was marked
by pageants and ceremonies among which was the unveiling of a
plastic flame on O'Connell Bridge – 'The Tomb of the Unknown
Gurrier', as the *Irish Times* satirist Myles na Gopaleen (then at the
height of his fame) dubbed it. Unknown gurriers were also responsible for smashing Clerys' windows on a night of violence during
which the flame was consigned to the bed of the Liffey.

For Clerys itself that year marked the centenary of the store and
a chance to look back over its chequered history. The growth of the
firm, despite all the difficulties over the years, had been continuous

and impressive. There was little doubt among the staff that under Denis Guiney it would continue.

Many of the smaller drapery stores employed only women. The members of the Drapers' Association were therefore reluctant to meet claims for higher wages largely originating with the men employed in the larger firms such as Clerys. They spoke out warmly on the subject; and they had the support of Denis Guiney, who was one of those among the more prominent employers 'hot enough under the collar to talk rather strongly and give encouragement to the right-wing element of small employers', even though he undoubtedly had no wish to see the staff of Clerys on a picket. Wiser counsels eventually prevailed and talks were entered into. The No. 15 Branch of the Irish Transport and General Workers' Union (founded by James Larkin) was particularly strong in the larger wholesale and retail drapery firms, and observed closely any advances made by those in rival unions.[2]

The worst year of the decade was 1955, when, in addition to industrial unrest, unemployment and massive emigration reached alarming levels. Furthermore, though many small companies catered to the Irish market – firms such as Urney's and Lemons in sweets, Wills's tobacco, Donnelly's sausages, Gateaux cakes – they had to fight against the mounting imports from Britain and America. New policies were clearly needed. Here too Clerys had a role to play. The store's restaurant had become by this time 'something of a Fianna Fáil clubhouse'. On 16 October 1955 at a public dinner given there for members of the Fianna Fáil party, Seán Lemass, the shadow Minister for Industry and Commerce, outlined a new departure in public finance for development. This speech, which received great attention, though not reported initially in the party paper, the *Irish Press*, came to be dubbed 'The Clerys Ballroom Speech'. Lemass spoke of the need to create 100,000 jobs. This was to be achieved by investment programmes which would involve combining a government fund of £67 million with national savings to create private enterprise jobs. Though vague on detail, the speech had immediate effect.[3]

The emphasis would have to lie with exports. These had peaked in 1929 with £47 million, a figure which was not to be surpassed until 1960. The essential role of exports was realised after the Second World War. From 1946 Denis Guiney himself had been the director of an import/export company; and had for many years understood the need to sell in Europe. He was therefore well aware of the many problems Ireland faced in this area.

Lemass was speaking that night as an opposition leader. In 1957 his party Fianna Fáil were returned to power after the failure of the second inter-party government. There now began a crucial period for Lemass and for Irish industry. John Leydon, the permanent secretary of the Department of Industry and Commerce, whose thinking was much admired by Lemass, was a key figure here, in developing not only the industrial base, but also the larger elements of distribution and so on which were equally important. Guiney's achievements since 1932 had earned the respect of Lemass, who spoke warmly of him: 'He had known Mr Guiney for many years and had a very high regard for him both in relation to his exceptional business acumen and his general outlook on national affairs, which was very constructive.'[4] A 'constructive outlook', in Fianna Fáil language, was one which agreed with party policy.

From the Clerys Ballroom Speech came the economic development plan of 1958, the brainchild of T. K. Whitaker, the senior civil servant at the Department of Finance. It is from the 'Clerys Speech' and the subsequent plans, and their fulfilment by a Fianna Fáil government headed by Seán Lemass himself, that the prosperity of modern Ireland, fragile though it may sometimes seem, has stemmed.

9 Clerys dressed over-all for Dublin's increasing prosperity

Clerys and the trading sector generally are labour-intensive, and an expansion of this area will always indicate an increase in general prosperity. The new plans were aimed at creating an industrial base for the country, but firms such as Clerys were not neglected. Denis Guiney then employed over a thousand people, no mean figure in Irish terms then or now.

This was a period when many survivors from the 1920s were still on the staff, but the 1920s was also the time when many of those who were now in senior positions made their start. In those days men went into jobs for life with companies. For women paid employment ended when they married – often to friends made at work in Clerys. Work conditions were then very different, with a more informal manner from management and yet stricter treatment of staff.

Guiney left most of his staff management to his associate Mr Reidy, who was a hard taskmaster. Guiney could thus afford to adopt a benign, relaxed, paternalistic approach to his employees, while Reidy saw to it behind his back that very few ever stepped out of line. Inevitably there were occasional conflicts of interest. Guiney once asked his staff to work from eight in the morning, instead of the normal opening time of nine o'clock. The staff refused to come in so early, but were to rue their stand against the boss when later he, in turn, refused to concede time off at Christmas.

The internal arrangements for the staff would seem odd by today's standards. For example, there was only one toilet each for men and women, no rest rooms, and no staff canteen. There were other odd little touches. A donkey and cart were kept for collecting items from the warehouse, which added a colourful, if often too colourful, touch to the local streets in the early mornings, but this was a leftover from earlier days. Yet the firm, as a whole, was in good shape to meet the tasks of the day.

By now Denis Guiney's own day was well established in its pattern. In the morning he would come in from the Howth Road, where he lived, and go into Guineys, where he would take account of the previous day and any problems that were outstanding. His well-known figure, these days running a little to stoutness, was instantly recognisable by his customers, his mournful expression belying a deep delight in everything that had to do with his business.

Then he would go on to Clerys, where his first task was to look over the previous day's takings from each department. In this way he kept an immediate eye on where business was good and where there were problems either in stock or in advertising. He would then make his rounds of the store, calling on departments, noting prices and reducing those of items that were not moving. His mind seemed capable of holding the price of every item in the store and how much he had paid for it. At sale time he would set the prices, and Frank McAuliffe recalled that when he went over them later in order to mark them, he had retained each one accurately in his head.

In the early days Guiney had made it one of his tasks to travel to England to see the goods for himself. Often (so it was claimed) he would buy up a warehouse of stuff. But sometimes things went wrong. Soon after the war, for instance, a consignment of welling-ton boots from Argentina simply fell apart. But then, they had not been inspected personally by Guiney. By buying this way, he had the tightest control of his prices, which he could vary as he liked on his daily inspection.

He would lunch in Clerys restaurant – on one occasion he is known to have bellowed to those lingering over their meals: 'Do you not know there are those of us waiting to eat!'

The day's inspection done, Guiney felt he could retire to the Beehive Lounge for a drink. There other, more social, aspects of his business life were conducted. He did not maintain an office in the accepted modern business-management sense, and visitors were often slightly bewildered at having to speak to him while he was signing the week's cheques in the stock room. He seemed to regard an office as a way of cutting oneself off from one's business, which might perhaps be true. When he arrived in the morning, his coat would be stowed under the counter at the Information Bureau desk. If anyone wanted to know if he was in the store, they checked at the desk rather than with his secretary. It was both wonderfully individual and effective. And the business showed it.

In 1955 Denis Guiney had increased the capital of the firm by £50,000 to £3m, and again in June 1958 by £50,000. The company assets were valued in 1965 at some £3m. Legal advice had been taken by the Guineys on protecting their assets by a special trust for their heirs, their many nieces and nephews. Their personal holdings in the Talbot Street shops were transferred to a company Denis Guiney Ltd (created in February 1952), and other matters carefully tidied up.

The Clerys of this period, during the 1950s, is the Clerys which most Dubliners of the older generation now remember from their childhoods. There were long counters of dark wood, with the glass-fronted cases behind them in which the clothes and goods were kept. The staff members were all dressed in formal clothes, the women in black dresses with white collars, and there were twice as many of them as there are now. Conversations about clothes or carpets were broken by the whoosh and clatter of the pneumatic cash system, as the change and receipt fell into the wire basket behind the counter. The tables in the main hall were piled with bolts of cloth. The renowned bargain basement, that happy hunting ground for items one could not afford at the full price, was always busy.

For a child it was often the smallest, least considerable thing that mattered. There were small Irish dolls made in plaster or wood, dressed in attractive Connemara costume. These were on sale over the silver counter, doubtless as souvenirs for Americans, but to many juvenile eyes they had a curious charm. At Christmas time there was Santa's grotto, a visit to which was a high point of countless childhood memories.

For others there must have been other attractions, such as an unaccustomed teatime treat in the restaurant before a film. The store retained an attractive old-fashioned air, while still providing the latest goods. Everyone in Dublin knew it was the only place to go in the city for clocks at keen prices. Or a bargain in those long-legged pink cotton knickers of immense size that made the washing lines of Dublin such a curious sight in those days.

But things were changing again. Fianna Fáil, much to Denis Guiney's delight, returned to power in 1957. De Valera was making moves to retire. Seán Lemass was coming into his own at last, breaking with the theological certainties of his party by uttering new economic heresies. Dr Whitaker was even then at work preparing his pivotal economic plan for the nation. With the coming of 1958, Ireland, and Clerys with it, entered a new and more progressive development, signalled by the election of Lemass as Taoiseach in June 1959. An era in the political and economic growth of the country was closing, and another opening.

CHAPTER 7

A Whole New Scene, 1960-7

I

In August 1960 Denis Guiney made out his last will. Surrounded by signs of changing times, he was making his own provision for the future of his fortune.

The prosperity, which seemed to elude Ireland, had reached America in the late 1940s and Britain in the early 1950s. The post-war lifestyle of plastic and nylon, a man-made paradise in contrast to the wood and wool of an earlier era, came to Ireland only late in that decade. Imported American and British magazines emphasised a new kind of lifestyle, based on new fabrics, electric kitchen appliances and aids, and washing machines. *Life*, *Look*, and the ever popular *Saturday Evening Post* revealed a material paradise that haunted the daydreams of countless housewives. In a country which was not completely electrified until the 1960s, this was an enviable vista of richness just beyond reach.

The 1960s seemed a period of sudden and drastic changes. The elevation of the liberal-minded Pope John XXIII in 1958, and his calling of a new Ecumenical Council of the Church, together with the election of President John F. Kennedy in 1960, seemed to indicate the arrival of a younger vigour in world affairs, as did the retirement of de Valera. The economics of the period were reflected in the opening of a national television service in 1960, and in such contemporary enthusiasms as the showbands, which filled the dance halls of the country with bouncing energy. Suddenly the emphasis was on youth.

The whole country seemed caught in a mind-whirling mix of vibrant new forces that seemed to affect every part of one's life. Some of this was American-inspired, much of it British, some of it, in the field of religion, straight from Rome. Some of it may also have been due to the arrival of a younger generation of university-trained journalists, who replaced the old guard of the 1930s on some newspapers.

For Clerys this meant new customers with new demands. A market based on young people with significant buying power from jobs in the expanding economy was now emerging. At first Irish youth were very conservative in their tastes. In the early 1960s young men still dressed largely in grey trousers and sports jackets, much as their fathers had done in the years between the wars. Cavalry twill was now the most daring alternative to flannel or blue serge. Perhaps this was because their mothers still bought their clothes. What Clerys sold reflected these conservative tastes of a conservative society. It does not pay, Denis Guiney knew, to be too far ahead of local taste, too extreme for the person who actually pays the bills.

Himself a conservative man, Guiney must have been dismayed at the emerging styles. It began with the girls, of course. The Junior Miss of the previous decade was transformed into the fashion-conscious teenager – or so one might have thought from trade advertisements. Girls now wore their hair in 'bouffant' style and dressed in skirts with huge starched underskirts. These, though no one would have said so then, in their extreme fashion bore some resemblance to the crinolines of the 1850s. (It should also be remembered that these young women were the granddaughters of the silk-stocking wearing, cigarette-smoking, 'jazz-dancing' girls of the 1920s who had so shocked a previous generation.) By 1963 some young men too were wanting the latest styles. Rock 'n' Roll, lamented by parents and preachers, brought with it a new culture and a new lifestyle based on the earning power of young people.

But it was a culture and lifestyle that was catered for by a rash of low-capital shops called boutiques, with a rapid turnover of a rapidly changing stock. Mary Quant had overwhelmed the Paris couturier. Within a very short time the dress habits of a lifetime changed. Mini-skirts brought with them light underwear and tights, smaller bras or none, a lightweight style for a lightweight culture.

It was a new climate that shook the traditional stores like Clerys. Denis Guiney, who had begun in quite a different era, when good value and good quality meant clothes that would last for years, and when a solid foundation meant exactly that (in the form of a corset and suspender belt), found himself facing into the age of micro-skirts and disposable paper knickers. Prices, which had been stable for so long, now started to rise. But young people, now more independent, and with more money to earn and to spend, seemed unaffected. Clerys, which claimed that some ninety per cent of its stock was Irish-made, reached the middle 1960s facing a difficult period of rapid change.

Yet it was with great pride that the store celebrated its silver jubilee under Guiney's new management in 1965. Some aspects of the store in those days are now quite changed. One of these was Clerys' Information Bureau (modelled on that in Selfridges, in London), then under the capable direction of Eileen Murphy. Some queries she fielded were easy: 'Where will I find New Street? . . . Can I have three stamps? . . . What bus do I take to Rathgar? . . . Is there a good picture on in town?'

Denis Guiney now employed directly over a thousand people, and Clerys had an annual turnover of £7m. The restaurant, a famous lunchtime attraction in Dublin, could seat a thousand people at a sitting, and serve up half a million meals a year. All his enterprises in the stores were making money. There were no loss makers allowed.

Building work was in progress at Clerys again. The older premises were being expanded, which would add some two and half
acres of extra floor space for selling and storage. But Guiney had to
admit that he was now too old to add more realms to his empire: 'I
think I have enough in what I have. I come into work every day still.
Not for long, mind you. A couple of hours at a time. But I'll keep on
coming in until I'm just not able. I have no thoughts of retiring yet.'[1]

That was in 1965, the firm's 25th anniversary under his management. The following year during the early morning of 8 March,
the IRA blew up Nelson's Pillar, to prepare, in their own special
way, for the approaching fiftieth anniversary of the Easter Rising of
1916. This coup removed from the scene a symbol of Dublin City
that had stood since 1808: 'The Pillar' was local parlance for the
city centre. Clerys' windows were damaged and replaced after the
initial blast. Theirs were the only ones to survive the second explo-
sion by the army to remove the stump of the Pillar. This was too
powerful and did further damage. However, Clerys had been wise
enough to take precautions.

That year also saw the death of the great satirist Myles na
Gopaleen, who had made a swipe or two at Clerys in his time, and
of Seán T. O'Kelly, the former President of Ireland, who had tried
in vain to save the store in 1916 from looters during the Rising. Both
belonged to a now passing era. During the bank strike in the summer of 1966 Clerys and Guiney's played their role in keeping mere
cash flowing through the city's economy.

In 1966 too an offer of £11m was made for Clerys, but was
refused by the board. As a return on Guiney's initial investment
this was a considerable sum. But it went little way towards a just
price for the firm. In 1960 the turnover had been £4½m; in 1966 it
had reached £10m.

Denis Guiney was now in his seventies. It was understood by
some of his admirers that as he approached the end of a long career

that Denis Guiney was to receive an honorary degree from the National University of Ireland (NUI) – they thought that few men were more worthy of such a public mark of distinction. This would seem to have been about the time that Derrynane reopened in the summer of 1967, but the degree was never formally conferred.[2]

His health, which had always seemed good, was now causing concern to his family and colleagues. He was found to be seriously ill, while on holiday in Ballybunion where he and his wife still patronised the Castle Hotel, though he looked to some as hardy as ever. In the middle of September 1967 he entered hospital. For the three weeks he was there his friends and staff waited anxiously; donations were collected among the staff in his shops for masses for his recovery. But the illness was too advanced.

On 8 October 1967 Denis Guiney died of carcinoma of the colon in the Mater Private Nursing Home at 36 Eccles Street. He was 74.[3] That lifelong regime of cigarettes and whiskey, as well as irregular and often fatty meals, had finally taken their toll.

When Denis Guiney had married Nora Gilmore in 1921, he had called himself a 'draper' – a nice old-fashioned term; now he was described on his death certificate more grandly as a 'business director'. The words were a measure of how far he had risen in the world during those 46 years.

From Kerry and from Dublin, from all over Ireland and Britain tributes were paid to him both as a businessman and as a personality.[4] 'His passing', wrote the editor of *Irish Industry*, Victor Kuss, 'has left a gap in industrial life which will not be easily filled . . . Our industrial progress over the years has shown his insight and confidence were more than justified . . . Many will agree that his policy of large turnover and small profits contributed greatly to both industrial progress and the economy of the country.'[5] It was not forgotten that his personal courage in 1940 had saved a great store, and that he had over the years given employment to perhaps some 6,000 people. This was no mean feat for a man who had begun his own working life as an apprentice draper behind the counter of Crowley's of Killorglin.

While most papers wrote about his achievements as a businessman, a specifically Catholic paper wrote about the void left 'in the hearts of many of the poorer citizens who at one time or another experienced his unobtrusive generosity . . .[Denis Guiney] had a genius for helping in a quiet, unostentatious way, but with a generosity that was full and satisfying'.[6]

The funeral mass was held in the Pro-Cathedral, which is the parish church of Clerys. It was attended by Eamon de Valera, the President of Ireland, by former Taoiseach Seán Lemass, and representatives of the Taoiseach and other ministers. Afterwards the cortege moved through O'Connell Street past Clerys, closed for the day, where the flag flew at half-mast. The street was full of Dubliners paying their last respects to 'Our Dinny'. He was buried with quiet ceremony in the same grave in Glasnevin Cemetery as his first wife, over which he had raised a large memorial surmounted by a statue of the Virgin Mary. At Clerys next day it was business as usual. The life of his great store had to go on.

II

In his will probated in August 1968 Denis Guiney left a personal estate of £113,950. The trustees for the estate were his old friends at the Munster and Leinster Bank.[7] Aside from a token holding of 100 shares in the *Irish Press*, de Valera's party newspaper, his estate largely consisted of his house, Auburn, and his share in the equity of Clerys and Guineys. He left small sums of money for masses for the repose of his soul (then a common Catholic practice) and to charity, but what remained went in equal shares to his wife Mary

Guiney, his brothers, sisters and in-laws, seven people in all. This will does not reveal the full extent of what he had once owned as settlements of property had been made back in 1957 and in 1960.

The only other director of the firms had been his wife, and the intention had been to protect the interests of their heirs. This probate was challenged, under the terms of the Succession Act (1965), that protect the interests of widows and surviving children, which resulted by 1971 in Mrs Guiney herself gaining full control over Clerys with 52 per cent of the shares.[8]

After her husband's death Mrs Guiney made no change in her way of life. The business still claimed most of her attention, and she took a special interest in the original Guiney store in Talbot Street. On 17 May 1974 she was standing near the main door there, discussing matters with Frank McAuliffe, a long-time associate of the Guineys, when a car bomb (one of three in the city that day) exploded in Talbot Street. They were thrown back into the shop, but were not injured. Across the city 25 people were killed and over 100 maimed or injured. Once more the violence of Irish history had intruded into the business life of the Guiney family.

She stayed on in Auburn, their old home on the Howth Road. But property developers were beginning to impinge on the district. She had a brief legal flurry with the developer of the site next door over property boundaries. Finally, in early November 1999, she sold it to a property developer Sean McKeon of MKN Properties for over £3.4m. The contents of the house, an extraordinary collection of furniture and other items built up since the house had been bought, were auctioned off. Apartments were built on the land behind the house, which was now renovated in the excessive modern way so common in Dublin, the whole becoming a 'gated community'.

Mrs Guiney moved to accommodation in Killester, at 12 The Meadows, further out along the Howth Road, backing on to St

Anne's Park, where care could be more conveniently provided for her. She lived simply, as she had when Denis was alive, with a devoted housekeeper. For her, as for Denis Guiney, family and firm came first. And as the two were, in this case, almost the same thing, there was little reason to look beyond them either for occupation or for pleasure. However, she still played a few rounds of golf every week and bridge in the evenings.

La veuve Guiney, even at her great age, continued to preside over the affairs of the great firm, which she inherited from her husband. It was a trust she intended to maintain, a tradition of service, which would be hard to match here or elsewhere. The appearance of the store had been modelled on Selfridges in London, and it also followed the Selfridge model of trading from one large store. If he had lived another twenty years, as he might well have done, Denis Guiney would have broken with that earlier model and undoubtedly followed Ben Dunne, an aggressive newcomer to the Irish retail scene, who opened a superstore in George's Street in 1960 and introduced two concepts new to Irish retailing: branding under the generic name of St Bernard, and the direct display of goods to customers without the help of a shop assistant.

As the city-centre department store began to face increasing difficulties, many argued that the day of the nineteenth-century department store was over. Out-of-town trading such as Ben Dunne established at Cornelscourt in 1966, or American-style shopping malls such as the Square in Tallaght or at Liffey Valley, accessible by car, seemed to be where the future of Guiney's kind of retailing would be found. But his wife and heirs did not think so at first. There are now branches of Clerys at the Square and furnishing and household outlets at Blanchardstown and Leopardstown, which the management sees as most innovative, though in setting these up the firm was following a trading trend, not creating one.

The scale of Irish commerce is now of international dimensions, and has moved beyond the grasp of a reclusive lady and her advisers. None of the family now works in the business. The exact size of the Guiney family fortune is unknown, but it is certainly in excess of £25m. As Denis Guiney's father had died worth a mere £86, this is an illustration of the Irish economy's total transformation in the course of the last half of the twentieth century.

By the autumn of 2001, Guineys in Talbot Street had retrenched its trading space, and Mrs Guiney, having rejected a management buyout of the firm led by Tom Rea, the then managing director and his associates, in her last years retained hold of a company that in the end may be worth more for its site value than its future business potential.[9]

The firm's old rivals, Arnott's in Mary Street and the reorganised (and relocated) Brown Thomas in Grafton Street, seemed to many to represent more dynamic shops, better adapted to the changing market. The arrival in Dublin of major British retailers also added a further dimension to retail competition which Denis Guiney had not known, and which his widow seemed ill-equipped to counter in her turn. Yet she still dominated the business and her extended family. The years passed.

Then in 2004, at the age of 103, Mary Guiney, still living in The Meadows, succumbed to bronchopneumonia ('the old person's friend') and was moved to Beaumont Hospital. There she passed away after ten days of illness on 23 August.[10] Her death certificate describes her, in the correct language of the twenty-first century, as 'Chairperson of Clerys'. In a private funeral she was interred with her late husband in Glasnevin Cemetery – in the same grave as his first wife Nora.

In the 37 years since her husband's death, Mrs Guiney had built up a personal fortune of her own in property and investments. Her net Irish estate, when finalised for probate in February 2006, came to €5,979,719. After some 22 personal and charitable bequests of various sizes, the residue was divided between her housekeeper and three close relatives. However, this estate did not include the stores: three discretionary trusts, established in November 1957 and April 1976, had already disposed of these, in the interests of an extensive network of heirs. Under the terms of her will and the trusts she had established over 90 relatives now came into their share of the total estate.

At Guineys in Talbot Street and at Clerys in O'Connell Street business went on.

Conclusion

I

For all his fame as a businessman, and for all his great wealth, Denis Guiney was essentially a private man of simple pleasures. Although he lived comfortably in a large and well-appointed Victorian mansion, this did not truly represent the real style of the man, as known to his friends and neighbours in north Dublin. He was happiest when having a drink with a pal in his local pub, Phil Byrne's, or when playing a round of golf on the nearby course at Clontarf. There was nothing ostentatious about him. He owned a car, but seldom used it, preferring to take a lift to work from any passing vehicle on the Howth Road that was going into the city; his figure was such a familiar one to Northsiders that he never had any difficulties. When he did take a bus, he would only pay with a £10 note now and again; the regular conductors on the route were happy to oblige him in this charming eccentricity. Similarly, he bought his daily newspapers at the local shop, paying with the occasional £10 note; he also invited the owner of the shop to bring her small children into Clerys at Christmas, where he gave them the run of the toy department to select gifts.

Denis Guiney was one of those whom charity organisers always knew would be a ready source of help, though this was often given privately. For instance, he lent his little two-roomed gate lodge at

Auburn to a newly recruited teenage civil servant from Valentia Island in Kerry, who had found it impossible to get affordable accommodation for herself and her mother in the city.[1] But his good works were not confined to Ireland. A Tipperary woman living in south-western France, where she served as housekeeper to a series of impoverished parish priests, was supplied on her visits to Dublin over many years with sets of clothes suitable for her abbés.[2] Help was also given to Catholic missions, such as the Mill Hill Fathers, the Jesuits and the Holy Ghost Fathers.

These and many others acts of great personal kindness were not publicised, but were widely known. Indeed, unlike so many businessmen of today, Denis Guiney had little taste for the limelight. Nevertheless, many clubs and sporting associations, especially the GAA, on the north side of Dublin were indebted to him for essential help when the need arose.

The Guineys had no children of their own. However, they maintained close contacts with the extended Guiney and Leahy families, and took a great interest in their many nieces and nephews. Denis also had a special affection for a god-daughter, the child of a friend of his youth who had died tragically young in an accident, and lavished much care and attention on her.

He had many passionate enthusiasms. He was a long-time supporter of the Fianna Fáil party, being, of course, from a part of the country where de Valera was seen more as a figure of national myth than a mere politician. Denis Guiney's politics were traditional, a part of the lifestyle not only of his own Kerry, but of rural Ireland as whole, that he brought with him to the city. Many Fianna Fáil and Old IRA events were held in Clerys' restaurant.

Nor was his home county of Kerry forgotten after all his years in Dublin. Local groups there benefited from his help, and we have already noted the unfortunate Derrynane Trust, which finally passed out of his hands at the end of 1964. He retained his interest in the affairs of the GAA. Under his aegis Clerys staff played for the Kickham Club, in which all the city drapers were involved. He still attended matches in Croke Park, and not only when the team from Kerry was playing.

Every year he and his wife would take a holiday in Ballybunion or with relatives in Kerry or Limerick. They never went abroad except on business. Spain and France held no attractions for either of the Guineys. An occasional pilgrimage to Lough Derg in Donegal would have been seen too as a special kind of vacation rather than a test of endurance.

Yet, for all his simplicity and personal modesty, Denis Guiney was that rare phenomenon, a national figure, a legend in his own lifetime. In 1950 the influential *Capuchin Annual*, then in its heyday, included him among its gallery of distinguished national figures, 64 in number.[3] It was an honour of a particular and special kind: he had been placed securely in the pantheon of the Irish Republic – a very different tribute to that so ironically paid to him eight years earlier by *The Bell*. For the 'Bellman' had been puzzled. 'Mr Guiney,' he mused, 'despite the blue eyes and the Kerry accent, with which you could thatch a comfortably sized cottage, leaves me hanging in the air, baffled, unresolved. The essential *Guiney qua non*, as you might say, still eludes me.'[4]

The essential Guiney was less of a puzzle to the rural imagination which recognises him as a familiar type, the country boy who puts one over on the smart city types. It is in this role that he has entered the supremely exclusive sphere of Irish folklore, featuring as a nimble-witted hero in the tales of traditional storytellers.[5]

To thus become a figure in the national *seanchas* places Denis Guiney in a class with the King of Ireland's son, St Patrick, Daniel O'Connell and Charles Stewart Parnell. What greater fame could any Irishman hope for?

II

The legend of Denis Guiney was one which his associates invoked
with awe. Frank McAuliffe, closely involved with running Clerys
and the store in Talbot Street as a director, and for many years a
friend and associate of Guiney, remembered him thus:

> I was fortunate to know this colossus of big business from my
> childhood years, and I have many happy memories of his visits to my
> uncle's farm in County Limerick. He gave me my first job, and in later
> years, when he appointed me fabric buyer in Clery & Co., I had the
> privilege of learning from him some of the finer points of merchan-
> dising. For fifty-five years Denis Guiney was a household name
> throughout Ireland. He was practising the techniques of bulk-buying,
> small profit-taking, quick turnover and high-powered advertising long
> before the chain store, discount store and supermarket came into being.
>
> He was a great supporter of Irish industry, and was always willing
> to give any acquaintance of his a helping hand in business. He gave
> generously to all charitable organisations, and never failed to contri-
> bute handsomely to his poorer customers who might be suffering
> financial difficulties at Holy Communion and Confirmation time. He
> never let money change his lifestyle, and never let success go to his head.[6]

In the Clerys of today, which marked the centenary of the name
in 1998, only a small part of the achievements of Denis Guiney can
be seen.[7] It has become less of a department store, and more a
location for concessionaires, such as international design labels.
The nineteenth-century department store has, in any case, largely
given way to the shopping mall, located in both the city centre and
in the outer suburbs, where parking is more readily available for the
car-driving population. The city centre had been for the pedestrian
and the carriage trade – the shopping centre is for those with cars.

When Guiney was alive he supported the GAA, as Clerys still does; but across the way Arnotts now boasts a Manchester United shop – an index of the change that has occurred. Even 8 December, that great pre-Christmas shopping day at Clerys for rural people coming up to Dublin, has become a thing of the past. Time and commerce have moved on.

III

Denis Guiney was very much a man of his era. He lived through a significant change in the commercial life of Ireland, a move from businesses which were very much created and controlled by one man to a period when large companies are operated by boards, shareholders and financial institutions.

He had begun his own working life in a small shop in a small country town, at a time when the majority of Irish people led rural lives with limited material prosperity. When he died, Ireland's interests had become largely urban, and an increasing material prosperity had opened up new opportunities for businessmen.

The energetic economy of today which has brought Ireland to twenty-first place in the table of world prosperity has created a country he would find unrecognisable, but also one full of great potential for business. As a transitional figure between these two ways of life, and whose own life and work played an important part in improving the lives of Irish people, Denis Guiney will always be of special historical significance.

Notes

Chapter 1: *Early Years, 1893–1908*

1   Batt O'Connor, *With Michael Collins in the Fight for Irish Independence* (London, 1929), p. 7. For further details see *Cork Hist. & Arch. Soc. Jn.*, 2nd Series, XXVI (1920), pp. 81–2; XXVII (1921), pp. 42–3.

2   According to local historian John O'Mahony in 1920.

3   *Dublin Builder*, 1 Oct. 1866, p. 243; *Irish Builder*, 1 Dec. 1868, pp. 295–5; T. J. Barrington, *Discovering Kerry* (Dublin, 1976), pp. 176, 230. See also Batt O'Connor, *With Michael Collins*, pp. 7–9, for his childhood impressions of the area.

4   A mission by Rev. Charles Gaynor and the former Catholic Thomas Moriarty was successful around Brosna in the years before the Famine: see Barrington, *Discovering Kerry*, p. 110.

5   John O'Mahony, 'History of Brosna', *Cork Hist. & Arch. Soc. Jn*, 2nd series, XXVI (1920), pp. 81–2, quoting Reid's *Travels in Ireland* (1822).

6   *The National Gazetteer: A Topographical Dictionary of the British Islands* (London, 1868), I, p. 397.

7   C. P. Crane, *Kerry* (2nd edn, London, 1914), p. 196.

8   Abstracted from the decennial *Censuses of Ireland*. See also *The Famine in Kerry*, (Kerry Archaeological and Historical Society, 1997).

9   Registration of birth, Tralee, 1893, vol. 5, p. 486, entry 301, September quarter. In some public records the spelling is Knockavinna. Further information on the Guiney family was collected orally by Frank McAuliffe.

10   Albert Casey (ed.), *O'Kief, Coshe Mang, Slive Lougher and Upper Blackwater in Ireland* (Birmingham, Alabama, 1952–71), VI, p. 277.

11   It had a Poor Law valuation of £5 15s, a redemptive value of £65, and was valued for estate duty in 1930 at £78 15s (Probate record with grant of administration of estate of Cornelius Guiney, 1931).

12 *Census of Ireland* 1901, Kerry 139/ D. E. D Gneeves, 6: Knockawinna, form 16; *Census of Ireland* 1911, Kerry 139/ D. E. D. Gneeves, 6: Knockawinna, form 13. Jeremiah King, in *County Kerry, Past and Present: A Handbook to the Local and Family History of the County* (Dublin, 1931), lists some 17 Guiney families in the county from the Census of 1901. On the form for 1901 it is stated that Cornelius was 56 (born 1855) and Julia 36 (born 1865); while on the 1911 form, when pensions were in the offing, he was 62 (born 1849), and she was 50 (born 1861). As all these dates are largely before the introduction of registration in 1864, this variation is hardly surprising. His death certificate (1929) says he was 76 (and so born in 1852). Probably he was nearer 80.

13 Samuel Lewis, 'Brosna' in *A Topographical Dictionary of Ireland* (2 vols, London, 1837), I, p. 226.

14 S. M. Hussey, *The Reminiscences of an Irish Land Agent* (London, 1904), p. 214.

15 O'Connor, *With Michael Collins*, p. 13.

16 Valerie Bary, 'Mount Eagle Lodge' in *Historical and Architectural Notes on Some House of Kerry* (Whitegate, 1984).

17 Ibid., p. 120; see also *The Times* (London), 1–8 April 1882, and other papers of same dates; Hussey, *Reminiscences*, pp. 226–7.

18 T. M. Donovan, *A Popular History of East Kerry* (Dublin, 1931), pp. 96, 154–6.

19 Hussey, *Reminiscences*, p. 227.

20 O'Connor, *With Michael Collins* (1929), pp. 47–8; Donovan, *East Kerry*, p. 155

21 *The Kerryman*, 12 June 1920; see also J. A. Gaughan, *Listowel and Its Vicinity* (Cork, 1973), pp. 343–431, for the general local background to this period.

22 O'Connor, *With Michael Collins*, p. 49. Aeneas C. Guiney died in March 1936.

23 Dorothy Macardle, *Tragedies of Kerry* (Dublin, 1923).

24 *Sunday Press* (Dublin), 21 Mar. 1965.

25 For an account of a similar business in similar circumstances, see Charles Hughes: *Lankill to Westport 1876–1949*, by Harry Hughes and Áine Ryan (Westport, 2007).

26 Donovan, *East Kerry*, gives a vivid if sentimental view of the social background from 1880 to 1927.

27 John M. Synge, 'In West Kerry' [1907] in *The Aran Islands and Other Writings*, ed. Robert Tracy (New York, 1962), p. 253.

28 O'Connor, *With Michael Collins*, p. 13. O'Connor, who was born in July 1870, emigrated to America in October 1893; his impressions thus relate to the years from the opening of the Land War to the fall of Parnell and the split in the Irish Party.

29 Information from Mrs Maura Herson, formerly of Talbot Street, Dublin.

30 Lochlin MacGlynn in *The Kerryman*, 14 Oct. 1967.

31 Information on the Guiney family in part from interviews with Frank McAuliffe, who knew many of them from the 1940s onwards.

32 This is noted on the census form of 1911.

33 Donovan, *East Kerry*, p 191.

Chapter 2: *The World of Work, 1908–21*

1 Since the Education Act (Ireland) of 1892, third-class schools, intended for children destined for commercial or industrial life, rather than the universities or the professions, had required attendance only to the age of fourteen.

2 T. J. Barrington, *Discovering Kerry* (Dublin, 1976), p. 228; also Ward Lock Guides, *A Pictorial and Descriptive Guide to Killarney, the Kerry Coast, Glengarriff Cork, and the South-West of Ireland* (7th edn, London, 1926), p. 113.

3 *Census of Ireland* 1911, Kerry 80 / D.E.D. Killorglin, 24: Market Road, form 7.

4 See the description in Synge, 'In West Kerry,' pp. 247–51; see also Máire MacNeill, *The Feast of Lughnasa* (Oxford, 1965), pp. 289–300, where the origins are discussed at length in relation to local history; Margaret Murray, *The God of the Witches* (London, 1926), pp. 37–9, with details from Mrs Percival-Maxwell, for supposed connection with ancient beliefs; and Muriel Rukeyser, *The Orgy* (New York, 1965), which fill out the social background of the town. Accounts of the affair contemporary with Guiney can be found in *Irish Monthly*, XXII (July 1894), pp. 373–5, and *Kerry Archaeological Magazine*, V (July 1919), pp. 59–62.

5 *Irish Monthly*, V (July 1894), p. 374.

6 Author's interview with Frank McAuliffe.

7 He suggested to a journalist in 1965 that he was twelve months in Kilrush, from February 1911 to February 1912 (*Sunday Press*, 21 Mar. 1965).

8 Information about Killorglin, and Kilrush and Killarney below, has been extracted from *Slater's Royal Directory of Ireland* (1894 edn).

9 See *Pictorial and Descriptive Guide to Killarney and the South-West of Ireland*, p. 131.

10 *Census of Ireland* 1911, Clare 104 / D.E.D. Kilrush: 1 Market Square.

11 Barrington, *Discovering Kerry*, pp. 199–200; *Pictorial and Descriptive Guide to Killarney and . . . the South-West of Ireland*, pp. 73–81. Accounts contemporary with Guiney can be found in the *Irish Monthly*, Sept. 1902, and the *Catholic Bulletin*, Sept. 1914, Oct. 1919.

12 *Census of Ireland* 1911, Kerry 74 / D.E.D. Killarney Urban: 18. Henn Street, form 1.

13 Pádraig Ua Cearbhaill, 'The Oireachtas – "Irish Week in Killarney"', *Catholic Bulletin*, IV: 9 (Sept. 1914), p. 615.

14 Ibid., p. 616.

15 Ibid., p. 617.

16 Michal Hand, 'Irish Success Stories: Denis Guiney', *Sunday Press*, 21 Mar. 1965.

17 The firm did not survive the Depression, one shop being sold off in 1930 and the other two changing hands the following year. Robert Holmes reopened in smaller premises in South Great George's Street, but did not survive the war.

18 Ward Lock Guides, *Dublin* (1922 edn), p. 61.

19 William O'Brien, 'A rainless Killarney', *Catholic Bulletin*, ix (Oct. 1919), p. 513.

20 See also the discussion of this transition period in Peter Costello, 'The shape of life' in *The Heart Grown Brutal* (Dublin, 1977), pp. 119–40.

21 See letter from Declan Dwyer of Sunbeam Wolsey, Cork, in *Irish Industry*, IX: 12 (Dec. 1941), p. 9.

22 *The Shell Guide to England*, ed. John Hadfield (London, 1970), pp. 672–3.

23 Batt O'Connor, *With Michael Collins in the Fight for Independence* (London, 1929), p. 48.

24 Shaun MacManus, 'A remarkable man' (unsourced cutting in Deirdre Quinn Papers).

25 Michael Laffan, *The Resurrection of Ireland: The Sinn Féin Party, 1916–1923* (Cambridge, 1999) and Brian Feeney, *Sinn Féin: A Turbulent Hundred Years* (Dublin, 2002) offer the most recent accounts of this process.

Chapter 3: *In Business for Himself, 1921–40*

1 In the marriage register she gave her father's name as Patrick and his occupation as farmer. The only Nora Gilmore traced was born on 8 May 1896 at Lakeview, Mount Bellew, County Galway, whose father was a ploughman. 'Farmer' is, of course, in Ireland an elastic term, but Denis's bride was older than some have reported; Guiney himself thought she was born about 1900.

2 Thom's *Dublin Directory* (1921 edn).

3 Marriage registration, Dublin North 1921, vol. 2, p. 476, entry 8, June quarter.

4 Thom's *Dublin Directory* (1922 edn).

5 Ibid., based on information gathered by October 1921.

6 Arnold Wright, *Disturbed Dublin* (London, 1914), p. 136.

7 *Ward Lock Guide to Dublin and Environs*, 1920–21 edn, p. 39; ibid., 1950 edn, p. 47.

8 Quoted in *The Kerryman*, 14 Oct. 1967.

9 So too were the premises of Cornelius Crowley, which stood on the corner

of Cathedral Street, almost beside the Hammam Hotel, where Cathal Brugha was in command, and outside which he was killed. The compensation records do not seem to have survived among unsorted papers in the National Archives; the figures quoted are taken from the press in 1924 and 1926.

10 In 1956 Denis and his second wife Mary Guiney formed Guiney & Co. Ltd to acquire the assets of the first firm.

11 Quoted in *The Kerryman*, 14 Oct. 1967.

12 Michael Hand interview, *Sunday Press*, 21 Mar. 1965.

13 *Irish Industry* I: 2, (Dec. 1932), p. 9.

14 T. Desmond Williams, 'Conclusion' in *The Years of the Great Test*, ed. Francis MacManus (Cork, 1967), p. 179; John Horgan, *Seán Lemass: The Enigmatic Patriot* (Dublin, 1997).

15 His estate was originally valued at £65 5s which included £10 for personal effects, £76 10s for livestock, tools, etc., and 80 acres of land valued at £78 15s which was not included in the final sum, which was reduced to £86 10s.

16 Denis Guiney and the accountant Cornelius Cremin were the executors of the probate granted on 28 November 1945.

17 The house was sold in late 1999 to a property developer for the sum of £4m (approximately €5,078,952): see chapter 7.

18 George O'Brien, 'Industries' in *Saorstát Éireann: Irish Free State Official Handbook* (Dublin, 1932), p. 148.

19 Registration of death, Dublin North 1938, vol. 2, p. 209, entry 230, March quarter.

20 The hope of attracting the eye of the boss persisted. When a journalist was trying to interview Guiney in December 1941, he was surprised to find he was out on the floor of the shop rather than in his office. Was this, he asked the refined young lady at the information desk, like the current Hollywood success, *The Devil and Miss Jones*, about a tycoon who takes a job incognito in his own store? 'And does he marry one of the girls in the end?' was her immediate response.

21 Registration of marriage, Dublin North, 1938, vol. 2, p. 321, entry 153, December quarter.

22 *Sunday Press* (Dublin), 21 Mar. 1965.

23 Father's status from marriage record; date of birth from data supplied to Companies Registration Office, April 1999.

24 Further information about the development of Clerys can be found in Peter Costello and Tony Farmar, *The Very Heart of the City: The Story of Denis Guiney and Clerys* (Dublin, 1992).

Chapter 4: *The Making of a Department Store*

1 The history of Clerys before Guiney is discussed in Peter Costello and Tony Farmar, *The Very Heart of the City: The Story of Denis Guiney and Clerys* (Dublin, 1992).

2 Further details of McSwiney are given in Peter Costello, *James Joyce: The Years of Growth* (London, 1992); Peter Costello and John Wyse Jackson, *John Stanislaus Joyce* (London, 1997); Emmet Larkin, *The Consolidation of the Roman Catholic Church in Ireland 1860–1870* (Dublin, 1987); Emmet Larkin, *The Roman Catholic Church and the Home Rule Movement in Ireland, 1870–1874* (Dublin, 1990).

3 See John Sproule (ed.), *The Irish Industrial Exhibition* (Dublin, 1854). Several classes of exhibits covered cottons, woollens and linen goods.

4 'The conditions of Dublin', *The Builder* (London), 3 May 1856, p. 4. The building's completion was the subject of some controversy between Butler and Caldbeck: see the record of a special council meeting of the Royal Institute of Architects in Ireland, Minutes of General Meetings, 4 Mar. 1853, pp. 114–15 (6 Sept. 1853).

5 M. B. Miller, *The Bon Marché, Bourgeois Culture and the Department Store 1869–1920* (London, 1981); Frank M. Mayfield, *The Department Store* (New York, 1949).

6 Further details in Mayfield, *Department Store*; Marguerite Aspinwall, 'Department Stores' in the *Encyclopedia Americana* (New York, 1966 edn), VIII, 701–701d; Bill Lancaster, *The Department Store: A Social History* (London and New York, 1995).

7 'Ireland: monster houses', *The Times*, 24 Jan. 1857. See David Thornley, *Isaac Butt and Home Rule* (London, 1964), p. 19, for background on Butt's career at this time.

8 Hancock published two pamphlets dealing with this problem, including *Is the Competition between Large and Small Shops Injurious to the Community?* (Dublin, 1851), which includes details about the development of the large stores in Dublin.

9 Frances Moffat, *I Too Am of Ireland* (London, 1985), p. 68.

10 Conal O'Riordan, *Adam of Dublin* (London, 1920), p. 2. Conal O'Riordan, *Adam of Dublin* (London, 1920), p. 2. For an account of the career of W. M. Murphy, see Thomas Morrissey SJ, *William Martin Murphy* (No. 9 in the Life and Times Series, Dundalk, 1997).

11 The Intoxicating Liquor Act, 1943 [No. 7 of 1943], section 20 (1). More details about this period can be found in Costello and Farmar, *The Very Heart of the City*, pp. 13–74.

Chapter 5: *The Proprietor of Clerys, 1940–9*

1 Much of the detail of this chapter draws on interviews with former staff of Clerys conducted in 1992.

2 *Irish Times*, 12 Sept. 1941, p. 4.

3 'The new Clerys', *Irish Industry*, XI: 9 (Sept. 1941), p. 16.

4 See 'Dr Lucey attacks industy', *Irish Industry*, X: 4 (Apr. 1942), p. 8; also *Irish Ecclesiastical Record*, 5th ser., LVIII: 5 (Nov. 1941), pp. 385–400.

5 *Irish Catholic*, 12 Oct. 1967, p. 1.

6 See Ronald Nesbitt, *At Arnott's of Dublin, 1843–1993* (Dublin, 1993), pp. 114–16.

7 Though the file of *Guiney's News* in the National Library is complete, the copy of *Guiney's Story Book* has been stolen.

8 Preface to fund-raising pamphlet, *Save Derrynane*, issued from Clerys in 1946, by Guiney (NLI, Ir. 9141, p. 57); 'Historic preservation', *Catholic Historical Review* 1 (1964), p. 90. See also an article by Benedict Kiely in the *Capuchin Annual* (1946–7), pp. 393–407.

9 See *Irish Catholic Directory for* 1948, pp. 700–2, for the text of Archbishop McQuaid's characteristic response to Guiney's proposal of a vote of thanks, seconded by Cecil Lavery, SC, for presiding at the meeting.

10 These well-informed comments are extracted from Lord Killanin and M. V. Duignan, *Shell Guide to Ireland* (London, 1962), p. 117; 2nd edn (London, 1967), p. 131; Barrington, *Discovering Kerry*, p. 285; see also *Oibre* 6 (1968), pp. 11–12, and the OPW guides to Derrynane House of 1981 and 1985.

Chapter 6: *Through Leaner Years, 1950–9*

1 *Irish Times*, 22 Oct. 1952.

2 Ronald Nesbitt, *At Arnott's of Dublin*, 1843–1993 (Dublin, 1993), pp. 144–6.

3 For the background see John Horgan, *Seán Lemass: The Enigmatic Patriot* (Dublin, 1997), pp. 164–8.

4 *Irish Times*, 9 Oct. 1967.

Chapter 7: *A Whole New Scene, 1960–7*

1 *Sunday Press*, 21 Mar. 1965.

2 Officials at the NUI told me that they could find no record of this matter.

3 Registration of death, Dublin North, 1967, vol. 2, p. 222, entry 376, December quarter. The death was certified by Dr James Delaney.

4 *Irish Times*, 9 Oct. 1967.

5   [Victor Kuss], 'Mr Denis Guiney – an appreciation', *Irish Industry*, XXXV: 11 (Nov. 1967), p. 3.

6   *Irish Catholic*, 12 Oct. 1967, p. 1.

7   Records of Probate from Principal Registry, date of grant of probate, 13 Aug. 1968 (National Archives, Dublin); with the Schedule of Assets, file No. 16931 / 1967 (13 Aug. 1968), vol. VII / 26 / 27. There were 28,000 £1 shares @ £1 in Clerys (1941), £28,000, and 53,750 preference £1 shares @ 15/6d, £41,656. The shares in the Irish Press Ltd were worth a mere £15. Auburn was valued at £18,325.

8   The course of these changes can be read in the filed annual reports in the Companies Registration Office, Dublin. For the further history of the store see Peter Costello and Tony Farmar, *The Very Heart of the City: The Story of Denis Guiney and Clerys* (Dublin, 1992), pp. 129–43.

9   Author's interview with Tom Rea, Mar. 1999.

10 Death record, Registrar-General's Office, registration number 1268024, Sept. 2004.

Conclusion

1   Information from Mrs Monica Henchy, Nov. 1999.

2   Information from the late Mrs Marion Litton, 1992.

3   Adolf Morath, 'A portrait gallery: Mr Denis Guiney', *Capuchin Annual*, 1950–1, p. 457.

4   'The Bellman', 'Meet Denis Guiney', *The Bell* III: 4 (Jan. 1942), p. 268.

5   For example, a story from the west Donegal *seanachaí* Micí Sheáin Néill Ó Baoill in the 1950s, recorded in *Maith Thú a Mhicí: Roinnt de Chuid Scéalta Mhicí Sheáin Néill, Ó Rann na Feirste*, ed. Seosamh Maguidhir (Belfast, 1956), pp. 38–9.

6   Quoted in Peter Costello and Tony Farmar, *The Very Heart of the City: The Story of Denis Guiney and Clerys* (Dublin, 1992), pp. ix–x.

7   Kim Bielenberg, 'Under the eye of Clerys' clock', *Irish Independent*, 13 Jan. 1998.

Select Bibliography

These sources include those which deal with the development of the department store and with the history of Clerys, as well as with the life and career of Denis Guiney. It does not include some sources mentioned only incidentally in the notes. Daniel Francis (Frank) McAuliffe, a long-time business associate of both Denis Guiney and his second wife Mary, and a director of Clerys & Co (1941) Ltd, has in preparation for the Guiney family a full-scale 'authorised biography', which will not be published in the foreseeable future. This will contain more material from family and private sources than has been made available to the present writer.

PERSONAL INFORMATION AND INTERVIEWS

Frank McAuliffe, Tom Rea and the late Arthur Walls, all of Clerys; Mr Frederick O'Dwyer; An Dúchas; Rev. Sir K. M. Nixon, SJ; Mr Noel Peart; Miss Jeanette Fitzgerald-Lombard; Dom Charles Fitzgerald-Lombard, OB; Mr Edward McGuire; Mr James McGuire, University College Dublin; Professor Emmet Larkin, Chicago; Mr Paul Ferguson, Map Department, Trinity College Dublin; Ms Lisa Shields; Ms Kathleen Walsh; Ms Máiréad Dunlevy, formerly of the National Museum of Ireland; Mrs Maura Herson; Mrs Monica Henchy; Mrs Mrs Marion Litton; Tim Hannon; past and present staff of Clerys and Guiney's; and other informants who wish to remain anonymous.

MANUSCRIPTS AND ARCHIVAL MATERIALS

National Archives

M 3723 Clery Minors 1900–18
Census Returns 1901 and 1911 for Brosna, Killorglin, Kilrush, Killarney, Lower Sackville Street and Earl Place

Records of wills of Peter Paul McSwiney [1884], George Delany [1906], William Martin Murphy [1919], M. J. Clery [1898], Robert Clery [1900], Denis Guiney [1968]

Fenian Papers and Photographs of Suspects

Registrar-General of Ireland

Records of births, death and marriages, 1893–2004

Companies Registration Office

Guiney & Co (acquired 1956 by next)
Guiney & Co. Ltd
Clery & Co. (1941) Ltd
Denis Guiney Ltd (registered 1952 to acquire next)
Talbot Street Furnishing Co. Ltd
Denis Guiney Furnishing Ltd
Beleir Ltd (dissolved 1961)

Other Sources (all in Dublin)

Arnotts of Dublin, surviving records and memorabilia
Clery & Co., surviving records and memorabilia in hands of present company
Clery & Co. (1941), papers and records
Frank McAuliffe collection, Clontarf
Irish Architectural Archive records
Deirdre Quinn Papers
Royal Institute of Architects in Ireland, *Council and Committee Books*, 1853
William Caldbeck's *Account Book*, courtesy David Dickson, Department of Modern History, Trinity College Dublin
Edward McGuire Papers, courtesy James McGuire, School of History and Archives, University College Dublin
The Valuation Office, Dublin
The Registry of Deeds
Office of Public Works / National Parks and Monuments Service

Files of the *Irish Times*, *Irish Independent*, *Irish Press*, *Irish Catholic* and *Kerryman*

GUINEY PUBLICATIONS

Guiney's News (Dublin), 12 May 1941–4 Aug. 1947.
Guiney's Story Book, with Pictures for Painting, 80 pp (Dublin, 1945).

BOOKS AND ARTICLES

Adburgham, Alison, *Shops and Shopping, 1800–1914* (2nd edn, London, 1989).

Andrews, C. S., *Dublin Made Me* (Dublin and Cork, 1979).

Andrews, C. S., *Man of No Property* (Dublin and Cork, 1982).

Aspinwall, Marguerite, 'Department Stores' in *Encyclopedia Americana* (New York, 1966 edn), VIII, 701–701d.

Barrington, T. J., *Discovering Kerry, its History, Heritage & Topography* (Dublin, 1976).

Bary, Valerie, 'Mount Eagle Lodge' in *Historical Genealogical Architectural Notes on Some Houses of Kerry* (Whitegate, Co. Clare, 1984).

'The Bellman', 'Meet Denis Guiney', *The Bell*, III: 4 (Jan. 1942), pp. 268–76.

Bielenberg, Kim, 'Under the eye of Clery's clock', *Irish Independent*, 13 Jan. 1998.

Briggs, Asa, *Victorian Things* (London, 1988).

Caulfield, Max, *The Easter Rising* (London, 1963).

'Clerys of Dublin', *Irish Industry*, Supplement, IX: 11 (Nov. 1941).

Coffey, Thomas M., *Agony at Easter: The 1916 Rising* (London, 1970).

Comerford, C. V., *The Fenians in Context* (Dublin, 1986).

Costello, Peter, with Tony Farmar, *The Very Heart of the City: The Story of Denis Guiney and Clerys* (Dublin, 1992).

Craig, Alan, *Derrynane: A Short Guide to the Home of Daniel O'Connell* (Dublin, [1980]).

Craig, Maurice, 'The account-book of William Caldbeck, architect', *Architectural History*, XXVII (1984), pp. 423–7.

Crane, C. P., *Kerry (The Little Guides)* (2nd edn, London, 1914).

Cruickshank, Dan, 'A friendly giant to help with the shopping', *The Independent* (London), 12 Feb. 1992 [on Selfridge's 80th anniversary].

Curriculum Development Unit (ed.), *Dublin 1913 – A Divided City* (Dublin, 1982).

Daly, Mary E., *Dublin, the Deposed Capital: A Social and Economic History, 1860–1914* (Cork, 1984).

Donovan, T. M., *A Popular History of East Kerry* (Dublin, 1931).

Eaton, Leonard K., *American Architecture Comes of Age* (Cambridge, Mass., 1972).

Ellmann, Richard, *James Joyce* (2nd edn, London, 1982).

Farmar, Tony, *A History of Craig Gardner & Co.: The First Hundred Years* (Dublin, 1988).

Feeney, Brian, *Sinn Féin: A Turbulent Hundred Years* (Dublin, 2002).

Fraser, W. Hamish, *The Coming of the Mass Market, 1850–1914* (London, 1981).

Gaughan, J. Anthony, *Listowel and its Vicinity* (Cork, 1973).

Georgian Society Records (Dublin, 1911).

Hancock, William Neilson, *Is the Competition between Large and Small Shops Injurious to the Community?* (Dublin, 1851).

Hancock, William Neilson, *Is Distinct Trading or the Monster House Most Conducive to Public Interests?* (Dublin, 1859).

Hand, Michael, 'Irish success stories – Denis Guiney', *Sunday Press*, 21 Mar. 1965.

Horgan, John: *Seán Lemass: The Enigmatic Patriot* (Dublin, 1997).

Hughes, Harry with Áine Ryan, *Charles Hughes, Lankill to Westport 1876–1949* (Westport, 2007).

Hussey, S. M., *The Reminiscences of an Irish Land Agent* (London, 1904).

Industries of Dublin: Historical, Statistical, Biographical (London, [1888]).

Irish Industrial Exhibition (Dublin 1853) [catalogue].

Joyce, James, *Ulysses* (new edn, London, 1961).

Kelly's Directory of Ireland (London, 1905).

Keogh, Dermot, 'William Martin Murphy and the origins of the 1913 lockout', *Capuchin Annual*, 1977, pp. 130–58.

Killanin, Michael with Michael V. Duignan, *The Shell Guide to Ireland* (2nd edn, London, 1967).

[Kuss, Victor], 'Mr Denis Guiney – an appreciation', *Irish Industry*, XXXV: 11 (Nov. 1967), p. 3.

Michael Laffan, *The Resurrection of Ireland: The Sinn Féin Party, 1916–1923* (Cambridge, 1999).

Lancaster, Bill, *The Department Store: A Social History* (London and New York, 1995).

Larkin, Emmet, *James Larkin* (Cambridge, Mass., 1965).

Larkin, Emmet, *The Consolidation of the Roman Catholic Church in Ireland, 1860–1870* (Dublin, 1987).

Larkin, Emmet, *The Roman Catholic Church and the Home Rule Movement in Ireland, 1870–1874* (Dublin, 1990).

Lewis, Samuel, *A Topographical Dictionary of Ireland* (2 vols, London, 1837).

Litton, Helen, *The World War II Years: The Irish Emergency An Illustrated History* (Dublin, 2001).

[McEvoy, P. L.], 'Twelve years' progress', *Irish Industry*, I: 2 (Dec. 1932), p. 9.

MacGlynn, Lochlinn, 'Dublin's affectionate farewell to Denis Guiney', *The Kerryman*, 14 Oct. 1967, p. 12.

McManus, Shaun, 'A remarkable man' (unsourced cutting, Quinn Papers).

Mayfield, Frank M., *The Department Store* (New York, 1949).

Meenan, James, *The Irish Economy since 1922* (Liverpool, 1970).

Miller, Michael B., *The Bon Marché: Bourgeois Culture and the Department Store, 1851–1931* (London, 1981).

Moffat, Frances, *I Too Am of Ireland* (London, 1985).

Morath, Adolf, 'National Portrait Gallery: Denis Guiney', *Capuchin Annual*, 1950–1, p. 457.

Morrissey, Thomas, *William Martin Murphy* (Dundalk, 1997).

Mundow, Anna, 'Death of a lifestyle,' *Irish Times*, Weekend Supplement, 13 Jan. 1990.

Murray, Margaret A., *The God of the Witches* (London, 1926).

Nesbitt, Ronald, *At Arnott's of Dublin 1843–1993* (Dublin, 1993).

Norman, Edward R., *The Catholic Church and Ireland in the Age of Rebellion, 1859–73* (London, 1965).

O'Brien, Joseph V., *'Dear Dirty Dublin': A City in Distress, 1899–1916* (Berkeley, Calif., 1982).

O'Brien, William, *Recollections* (New York, 1905).

Ó Broin, Leon, *Fenian Fever* (London, 1971).

Ó Ceallaigh, Seán T. [Sean T. O'Kelly], *Seán T.* (Dublin, 1963).

[Ó Ceallaigh, Seán T.] O'Kelly, Seán T., 'Memoirs', *Irish Press*, beginning 3 July 1961.

O'Connor, Batt, *With Michael Collins in the Fight for Irish Independence* (London, 1929).

O'Dwyer, Frederick, *Lost Dublin* (Dublin, 1981).

Office of Public Works, National Monuments Branch, *Derrynane: Official Guide Book* (Dublin, [1970]).

Oram, Hugh, 'Fashioning stores for the future', *Irish Times*, 24 Jan. 1990.

Oram, Hugh, *The Advertising Book: The History of Advertising in Ireland* (Dublin, 1986).

O'Riordan, Conal, *Adam of Dublin* (London, 1920).

Rukesyer, Muriel, *The Orgy* (New York, 1962).

Save Derrynane Committee, *Cosnuighmís Doire Fhion-Áin. Save Derrynane* (Clerys, Dublin, [1947]).

Shaffrey, Maura, 'Sackville Street / O'Connell Street', *Irish Arts Review*, 1988, pp. 150–2.

Thornley, David, *Isaac Butt* (London, 1966).

Three Leaves from the History of a Great Irish Enterprise, 1853–1920 (Clerys, Dublin, 1920).

Wright, Arnold, *Disturbed Dublin: The Story of the Great Strike* (London, 1914).

INDEX